# LENT IN 50
## MOMENTS

# LENT IN 50 MOMENTS

*Fifty daily reflections from*
*Ash Wednesday to Easter Wednesday*

## LIAM KELLY

*With illustrations by Ted Harrison*

DARTON·LONGMAN+TODD

First published in Great Britain in 2021 by
Darton, Longman and Todd Ltd
1 Spencer Court
140–142 Wandsworth High Street
London SW18 4JJ

ISBN: 978-1-913657-32-1

A catalogue record for this book is available from the British Library.

Designed and produced by Judy Linard
Printed and bound in Great Britain by Bell & Bain Ltd, Glasgow

# Contents

# INTRODUCTION

A good number of years ago, so the story goes, a bishop decided that instead of writing the occasional pastoral letter to be read to the faithful, he would record his text on a cassette (yes, the story is that old!). This could then be played in church, a clear benefit being the privilege of hearing the bishop's own voice. One Sunday, the priest dutifully played the cassette at the first Mass and rewound it in preparation for the second, at which he announced to the assembled throng 'Now we have a pastoral letter from our bishop' and pressed the play button.

'Christ, it's Lent again!' the bishop's voice boomed around the church. Of course, had the priest carefully rewound the cassette right to the beginning, the bishop's heartfelt greeting to 'My dear brothers and sisters in Christ' would have been a more appropriate introduction to the season.

Yes, it is that time of year again. Those little creme eggs have been in the shops since Boxing Day, tempting us to focus our minds – or rather our stomachs – on the important message of consumerism: Easter is about Easter eggs, Easter bunnies and a nice Easter Sunday lunch.

But although supermarkets begin their Easter marketing the day after Christmas, the churches set aside a special period of preparation which is not about calorie-counting and watching the waistline, but about preparing spiritually for *the* great Christian feast of Easter. Welcome to Lent!

## WHAT'S IN A WORD?

The word Lent comes from the Anglo-Saxon word for springtime, *lencten*. The month of March was *lencten monath*, the month in which the days lengthened after the winter solstice. Since most of what we now call Lent falls in March, the Lenten fast became known as *Lencten-faesten*, or Lent.

## WHAT'S IN A NUMBER?

Fasting was an early Lenten theme in the Christian world and in the second century Christians prepared for Easter by fasting for two days. Over time, this was extended to the whole of the week leading to Easter. Fasting became associated with the number forty, echoing Jesus' fast in the desert (Matt. 4:2), Moses' time on Mount Sinai (Exod. 34:28) and the time spent by the Israelites in the desert. Eventually, the season of Lent itself was determined to be forty days.

But is it? Holy Thursday evening is the start of the Triduum (three days), a period of more intense preparation leading up to the celebration of Easter. So the start of Lent was counted back to the First Sunday of Lent. But Sundays were always considered to be the day of resurrection when no fasting should be undertaken, and so they did not count. So by the seventh century the start of Lent was anticipated to Ash Wednesday and included Good Friday and Holy Saturday to make up the numbers, so to speak.

So where does it all begin and end, do Sundays count, and are there forty days after all?

Lent officially begins on Ash Wednesday and ends at the start of the Easter Triduum on the evening of Holy Thursday. Sundays are included as part of Lent, as explained by the Catholic Church's *Universal Norms for the Liturgical Year and Calendar*: 'The forty days of Lent run from Ash Wednesday up to but excluding the Mass of the Lord's Supper' (n. 28); 'The Sundays of this time of year are called the First, Second, Third, Fourth, and Fifth Sundays of Lent. The Sixth Sunday, on which Holy Week begins, is called "Palm Sunday of the Passion of the Lord"' (n. 30).

So that is nice and clear: Lent should have forty days and counting every day from Ash Wednesday to Holy Thursday gets you to forty-four; if you take out the Sundays, you are left with thirty-eight. Maybe we should just leave the mathematics out of Lent!

## LENT IN 50 MOMENTS

So why *Lent in 50 Moments* when I could have gone for forty-four or thirty-eight? Lent has no meaning in itself. On Ash Wednesday in 2021 Pope Francis said 'We are now embarking on our Lenten journey, which opens with the words of the prophet Joel. They point out the path we are to follow. We hear an invitation that arises from the heart of God, who with open arms and longing eyes pleads with us: "Return to me with all your heart" (Joel 2:12). Return to me. Lent is a journey of return to God.'

As for any journey, we need signposts and guidance to help us find the route home. In this book that guidance is provided by daily reflections on passages of scripture. *Lent in 50 Moments* offers reflections which cover Lent, the Easter Triduum and the start of Eastertide itself, with the celebration of Easter Sunday, Easter Monday – *Pasquetta*, 'little Easter', as it is known in Italy – Easter Tuesday and Easter Wednesday, where our journey culminates by accompanying the disciples on the road to Emmaus and the encounter with the Risen Lord. The whole period is one journey in faith and reflection. A restaurant critic who confessed not to be staunchly religious once explained to her partner that 'Jesus went to the wilderness to fast and prepare for ministry, which is why I've given up sweet things'. But as Pope Francis said, 'Lent is not just about the little sacrifices we make, but about discerning where are hearts are directed. This is the core of Lent: asking where our hearts are directed. Let us ask: Where is my life's navigation system taking me – towards God or towards myself?'

The journey through Lent and Eastertide contained in this book provides a number of moments for reflection each day: a drawing of a particular object or occasion; the biblical references for the readings at Mass in the Catholic Church, with the Sunday readings taken from Year C of the Catholic Lectionary; a short commentary on the drawing and the biblical texts; and a final quotation and question for prayerful reflection.

## HOW TO USE THIS BOOK

This book is a journey. It can be read individually or used as part of a group discussion. It is important to bear in mind that any discussion in a group setting should be founded on respect and sensitivity; it should not become a dialogue of the deaf or even less a shouting match. Honesty, openness, a willingness to listen and learn can lead to fruitful dialogue. Throughout the text there are questions for reflection and, if you are in a group, for sharing (if you wish – no one should be forced to speak). The questions are not about making sure you get the right answers. This is not an exam. They are there simply to stimulate thought and reflection with those who are companions on the journey through Lent and Eastertide.

## GROUND RULES FOR GROUPS

- Speak if you want to, not because you feel you have to.
- Say what you want, not what you think others might want to hear.
- Listen with respect to the contributions of others.
- Respect the confidentiality of the group so that yours is a safe place to be honest.

Have a happy Lent!

# ASH WEDNESDAY TO THE SATURDAY AFTER ASH WEDNESDAY

# ASH WEDNESDAY

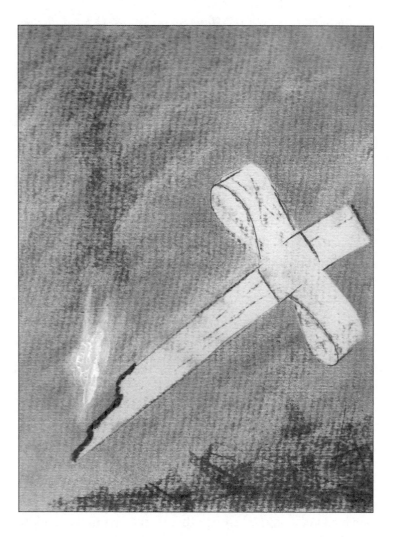

*Palm crosses are made from palms from* Hyphaene coriacea, *a small species also called the Lala Palm, which grow wild in the Masai area of southern Tanzania and other areas of eastern and southern Africa. The palms are dried, cut into strips and woven into palm crosses.*

*Joel 2:12–18 Tear your hearts and not your clothes*

*Psalm 51:3–6, 12–14, 17 Have mercy on us, O Lord, for we have sinned*

*2 Corinthians 5:20 – 6:2 Be reconciled to God ... now is the acceptable time*

*Matthew 6:1–6, 16–18 Your Father who sees all that is done in secret will reward you*

Primary school Masses on Ash Wednesday were always memorable, leaving you with a dirty big grey smudge on your forehead that you dare not wash off. It was almost like a badge of honour, showing that you had been 'ashed'.

Nearly thirty years later, and it was my turn to get things ready for the Ash Wednesday Mass. Vestments, OK; Mass books, OK; holy water for blessing the ashes, OK ... but where were the ashes? How did I get hold of ashes?

The easy answer is that they usually come in a nice little plastic sample bag from church suppliers. The reality is that they are the burned remains of the palm branches used the previous year. How ironic that the main item associated with Ash Wednesday is actually palm crosses from the previous Palm Sunday. Fortunately, I managed to find some leftover palms and burn them in time. A prayer of blessing says 'Bless this fire as it changes these branches of triumph into ashes of penance. As we move through these forty days in the shadow of the Cross, may we never lose sight of the Resurrection.'

But Ash Wednesday is not about badges of honour. Lent is not about telling everyone how charitable I am, how holy I might become, how good I am at fasting. It is about setting out on a journey to Easter with the Lord almost as a secret companion: 'Your Father, who sees all that is done in secret, will reward you' (Matt. 6:4).

I wish everyone a good journey in this Season of Lent. And I recommend a fast, a fast which will not make you hungry: a fast from gossip and slander. It is a special way. This Lent I will not speak ill of others, I will not gossip. And we can all do this, everyone. This is a good fast. And do not forget that it will also be helpful to read a passage of the gospel every day, to carry a small gospel in your pocket, in your purse, and pick it up when you can, any passage. This will open the heart to the Lord.

Pope Francis, 28 February 2021

**In the Second Letter to the Corinthians, Saint Paul says, 'See, now is the acceptable time; see, now is the day of salvation.' In what way is Lent the acceptable time?**

# THE THURSDAY AFTER
# ASH WEDNESDAY

*In 1527, the German artist Hans Holbein the Younger was commissioned to paint Sir Thomas More. Holbein lived in London at the time and befriended More, who lived in what became known as Beaufort House in the Chelsea area, on present-day Beaufort Street. More and his family were regular worshippers at Chelsea Old Church. The Holbein portrait is in the Frick Collection art museum in New York.*

*Deuteronomy 30:15–20 I am offering you life or death, blessing or curse*

*Psalm 1:1–4, 6 Blessed the one who has placed all trust in the Lord*

*Luke 9:22–25 Whoever loses life for my sake, will save it*

My first involvement in drama at school was when I was given the glorious role of Prompter in a production of Robert Bolt's *A Man for All Seasons*. I am not sure if this was the thespian equivalent of always being picked as goalkeeper in football, but I enjoyed it!

*A Man for All Seasons* is the story of Sir Thomas More, Lord Chancellor of England, who refused to sign a letter asking Pope Clement VII to annul King Henry VIII's marriage to Catherine of Aragon. One of the people who provides damaging information about Thomas More is Richard Rich, who is made Attorney General of Wales as a reward. I remember vividly the brilliant line uttered by More at his trial after listening to Rich's evidence: 'For Wales? Why Richard, it profit a man nothing to give his soul for the whole world … but for Wales?'

Thomas More, canonised by the Catholic Church in 1935, and Richard Rich, who was Lord Chancellor from 1547 to 1552, are interesting Lenten figures, for the choices they made are those at the heart of a life of Christian faith and action.

The stark reality of that choice, addressed to us today in a far more dramatic fashion than in any theatre production, is stated very clearly in today's readings. In the book of Deuteronomy, Moses says to the people 'Look, today I am offering you life and prosperity, death and disaster' (30:15); in Luke's Gospel, Jesus says 'For whoever wants to save life will lose it; but whoever loses life for my sake, will save it. What does it profit someone to gain the whole world while losing or forfeiting self?' (9:23–25).

> *The sin of worldliness is a preoccupation with the things of this temporal life. It's accepting and going along with the views and practices of society around us without discerning if they are biblical. I believe that the key to our tendencies toward worldliness lies primarily in the two words 'going along'. We simply go along with the values and practices of society.*
>
> Jerry Bridges, *Respectable Sins: Confronting the Sins We Tolerate*

**Thomas More was not willing to compromise his beliefs and remained steadfast unto death. On the scaffold, he said, 'I die the king's good servant, and God's first.' Is there any compromise in how you live out your faith?**

# THE FRIDAY AFTER ASH WEDNESDAY

*The Holy or Jubilee Door of St Peter's Basilica, Rome. The doors, designed by Vico Consorti and cast in Florence, have sixteen bronze panels portraying scenes of sin and redemption. The door is cemented shut and opened for the designated Jubilee Years, when pilgrims flock to Rome and enter the Basilica by the Holy Door, a symbol of entering into the presence of God.*

*Isaiah 58:1–9 Is not this the sort of fast that I favour?*

*Psalm 51:3–6, 18–19 A broken and humbled heart, O God, you will not spurn*

*Matthew 9:14–15 When the bridegroom is taken away from them, then they will fast*

Pope Francis decreed the year 2016 to be an Extraordinary Jubilee of Mercy, running from 8 December 2015, the Feast of the Immaculate Conception, to 20 November 2016, the Feast of Christ the King (yes, I know the numbers do not quite add up – this 'year' has 349 days!). However, I am sure eyebrows were raised, maybe even heads were shaken, in the Vatican curia when it was announced that the Jubilee would not begin with the Pope's solemn opening of the magnificent bronze Holy Door in St Peter's Basilica, tapping three times while the verse 'Open to me the gates of justice' was sung. No, the focus was to be on Cathédrale Notre-Dame in Bangui, Central African Republic, where, on 29 November 2015, Pope Francis solemnly opened a wooden door designated as a Holy Door. Pope Francis chose Bangui to jump start the Holy Year because this was an active warzone, yet he called on people to arm themselves not with weapons but with righteousness, love and mercy, surely useful tools not just for the occasional Jubilee Year, or even the annual Lenten observance, but the day-to-day life of being a Christian.

In the Old Testament, the message of the Jubilee Year focused on liberation and the prophet Ezekiel actually calls it the 'year of liberation' (46:17). Restoration was at the heart of the Jubilee, a point echoed in Isaiah: 'Is not this the sort of fast that I favour: to open unjust fetters, to undo the straps of the yoke, to let the oppressed go free and to break every yoke? Is it not sharing your food with the hungry, bringing into your house the homeless poor, clothing one you see to lack clothing, not drawing back from your own kin?' (58:6–7). This is a more challenging fast than giving up biscuits.

> *The one who fasts, but does no other good, saves his bread but goes to Hell.*
>
> Italian proverb

**How do you perceive fasting during Lent?**

# The Saturday After Ash Wednesday

*The State Dining Room, Royal Yacht* Britannia. Britannia *was used by Queen Elizabeth II and the royal family for more than forty years and was decommissioned in 1997. Today, it is a major tourist attraction in the Port of Leith, Edinburgh. Many famous guests were hosted by the Queen in the State Dining Room. The table would seat a maximum of fifty-six for banquets, but superstitiously the Queen would only ever have an even number of guests, so that if someone dropped out or failed to turn up then someone else had to drop out, too.*

*Isaiah 58:9–14 Your light will rise in the darkness*

*Psalm 86:1–6 Teach me, O Lord, your way, so that I may walk in your truth*

*Luke 5:27–32 I have come to call not the righteous but sinners to conversion*

I once heard a discussion on BBC Radio 5 Live in which football pundits were discussing their ideal dinner guests. The majority of those invited were from the world of football: ex-managers to provide tactical inspiration, former players to talk about the best-ever goals, and so on. One of the reporters from Scotland suggested chef Gordon Ramsay might also have been a useful addition, since he had been on the books of Glasgow Rangers Football Club for six months, or Sir Alex Ferguson, who as a player toyed with the idea of opening a restaurant and got hands-on training at a restaurant next to Hampden Park in Glasgow before opening his own pub in Govan.

The discussion had been sparked by a guest list provided by a former international footballer in a club matchday programme. But rather than a table packed with former teammates and managers, his was far more interesting: Keith Richards of Rolling Stones fame ('my number-one dinner guest'), Joseph Stalin ('in the cabinet with Lenin and rises to power and rules with an iron fist'), Genghis Khan ('his leadership and ferocity is probably unmatched'), Chairman Mao ('Imagine uniting a community of a billion people') and Napoleon Bonaparte ('just fascinating'). Imagine trying to work out a seating plan for that group!

In Luke's Gospel, the Pharisees and Scribes complain about Jesus' dinner company, since he eats with tax collectors and sinners. Today, I suspect anyone arranging a dinner party invites people on merit: family, friends, and neighbours. The invitation from Jesus is very different. I am called by Jesus precisely because I am *not* worthy, because I am a sinner: 'I have come to call not the righteous but sinners to conversion' (Luke 5:32).

> *This is what God's kingdom is like: a bunch of outcasts and oddballs gathered at a table, not because they are rich or worthy or good, but because they are hungry, because they said yes. And there's always room for more.*
>
> Rachel Held Evans, American Christian author,
> 1981–2019

**Whom would you invite to a Lenten dinner? If you invited Jesus, what would you say to him?**

# THE FIRST WEEK
# OF LENT

# THE SUNDAY OF THE FIRST WEEK IN LENT

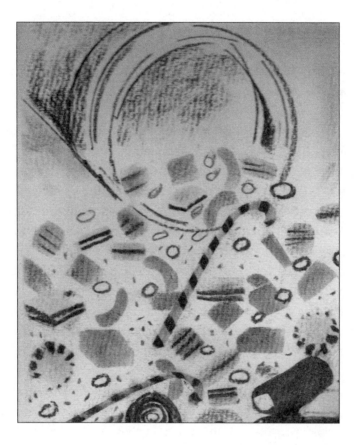

*The oldest sweet shop in England is located in Pateley Bridge in Nidderdale in the Yorkshire Dales. The shop was established in 1827 in a building dating back to the 1600s. The shop began selling sweets and luxury chocolates to local mill owners, quarry workers and labourers. Today, from rows of glass jars stacked high on the shelves, the sweet shop pilgrim will be able to buy humbugs, aniseed balls, pear drops, jelly babies, liquorice torpedoes and much more!*

*Deuteronomy 26:4–10 The creed of the chosen people*

*Psalm 91:1–2, 10–15 I will be with him in distress*

*Romans 10:8–13 The creed of the Christian*

*Luke 4:1–13 Jesus was led by the Spirit through the wilderness and was tempted there*

'I can resist everything except temptation,' said Oscar Wilde. Sweets have always been a temptation. My weekly pocket money of 3d – now probably worth about 25p – was usually spent on sweets at the wonderfully named The Penny Drink. Then Lent came along and I was told I had to give up sugar. Of course, my eight-year-old mind saw no problem with that: sugar was sugar, sweets were sweets – two totally different things! The error of my ways was quickly pointed out and it was made very clear that giving up sugar meant sweets too. Not to be outdone, I reasoned that this did not prevent me from buying sweets: I was simply not allowed to eat them during Lent. I happily stockpiled mountains to be consumed alongside too many Easter eggs!

Temptation is nothing new and being tempted to eat a few sweets is small fry, really. The gospel account of Jesus in the wilderness is not just a nice Lenten story to encourage us to persevere and not give in. The temptations Jesus faced are still a reality for us today: to satisfy our physical needs and desires; the achievement of great power; and defying or putting God himself to the test.

Whether it is a few wine gums when I have in fact given them up, or, at a completely different level, craving power and wealth, temptation is all about putting 'me' first, making 'me' the centre of the world. Jesus' response is clear: 'The Lord your God you shall worship and him alone shall you serve' (Matt. 4:10).

> *Jesus does not dialogue with the devil. Jesus responds to the devil with the Word of God, not with his own words. In temptation, we often begin to dialogue with temptation, to dialogue with the devil: 'yes, I may do this ... then I will go to confession, then this, then that ...' We must never dialogue with the devil. Jesus does two things with the devil: he either sends him away or, like in this case, he responds with the Word of God. Be attentive to this: never dialogue with temptation, never dialogue with the devil.*
>
> Pope Francis, 1 March 2020

**What are your worst temptations? What is your best antidote to temptation?**

# THE MONDAY OF THE
# FIRST WEEK IN LENT

*The tomb of Major General Charles George Gordon is to be found in St Paul's Cathedral, London. 'Chinese Gordon', or 'Gordon of Khartoum', was killed in 1885 and a statue of him was erected in Trafalgar Square in 1888. It was reinstalled on the Victoria Embankment in 1953.*

*Leviticus 19:1–2, 11–18 You shall administer justice to your fellow-citizen justly*

*Psalm 19:8–10, 15 Your words are spirit, Lord, and they are life*

*Matthew 25:31–36 In so far as you did this to one of the least of these brothers or sisters of mine, you did it to me*

Major General Charles George Gordon CB (1833–1885) was a British Army officer and administrator best known for his service in China in the 1860s. 'Chinese Gordon', as he was nicknamed, commanded the 'Ever Victorious Army' and played a significant role in putting down the Taiping Rebellion. Major Gordon declined all financial rewards offered to him by the Chinese Emperor but eventually accepted the title of Field Marshal of Jiangsu province, with permission to wear the imperial yellow jacket, a privilege bestowed on only forty individuals. In addition, a heavy gold medal was struck in his honour and given to him by the Empress Regent. It became his proudest possession.

Gordon was killed in Khartoum in 1885 and his tomb is in St Paul's Cathedral, London. After his death, the gold medal was nowhere to be found. Years later, it was discovered that Gordon had had the inscription removed and sent the medal to Manchester to help to buy food for people who were starving because of the Lancashire Cotton Famine. In his diary, he wrote 'The last and only thing that I had in this world that I valued I have given over to the Lord Jesus Christ.'

Jesus' vivid account of judgement recorded in Matthew's Gospel sees the separation of people into those who have served the needy and those who have not – they are classified among the sheep or the goats, headed for eternal life or eternal punishment. The criterion for judgement does not focus on flamboyant, extravagant generosity, but humble service of those in need: 'In so far as you did this to one of the least of these brothers or sisters of mine, you did it to me' (Matt. 11:45).

> *At the end of our life we will be judged on love, that is, on our concrete commitment to love and serve Jesus in our littlest and neediest brothers and sisters. That mendicant, that needy person who reaches out his hand is Jesus; that sick person whom I must visit is Jesus; that inmate is Jesus, that hungry person is Jesus. Let us consider this.*
>
> Pope Francis, 26 November 2017

**Major Gordon used to say 'You must give up your medal' to indicate the cost of giving up something important to you in order to help others. For whom would you give up your 'medal'?**

# THE TUESDAY OF THE FIRST WEEK IN LENT

*Praying Hands is a well-known pen-and-ink drawing by the German artist Albrecht Dürer (1471–1528), to be found today in Vienna's Albertina Museum. There are a number of theories about the origin of the drawing: its other title – Study of the Hands of an Apostle – suggests it may have been a sketch for the hands of an apostle whose complete figure would have been the central panel of a triptych in Frankfurt, the Heller Altarpiece, destroyed by a fire in 1729. Other theories have suggested the drawing is of the hands of his brother, Albert, or that Dürer modelled the hands after his own.*

*Isaiah 55:10–11 My word shall achieve what it was sent to do*

*Psalm 34:4–7, 16–19 The Lord rescues the righteous in all their distress*

*Matthew 6:7–15 Pray like this*

The most famous prayer is the one Jesus taught his disciples and which today we call the Our Father, the Lord's Prayer. Nearly fifteen years ago, an online satirical Christian magazine ran a competition to rewrite it for trendy texting on mobile phones, perhaps in an attempt to modernise this age-old message. The aim was to reduce the prayer from 372 characters to 160 or fewer, and the winning entry opened with the familiar salutation 'dad@hvn,ur spshl'. To bring matters right up to date, to mark World Emoji Day on 17 July 2019, the Archbishop of Canterbury tweeted the Lord's Prayer in emojis. In his tweet, he used a range of emojis including clouds to represent heaven, a halo in place of the word hallowed and a purple devil to signify evil.

There are many definitions and quotes about prayer, from the sublime (St John Damascene's 'Prayer is the raising of one's mind and heart to God or the requesting of good things from God') to the ridiculous ('Prayer: the world's greatest wireless connection' – but maybe this is profound too?). A definition tells you what something means, or, to use the dictionary definition of 'definition', it is a statement of the exact meaning of a word. A quick internet search for the word 'prayer' will give you more than thirty definitions.

In Luke's Gospel, Jesus responds to the request 'Lord, teach us to pray' by speaking to the disciples about the prayer we now call the Our Father. In Matthew, Jesus states first of all that prayer is not about using lots of words, deafening God with our non-stop verbose requests. Before anything else, prayer is a relationship, not a text or a tweet – a relationship with someone we are able to call our Father.

> *The intrinsic character of prayer is trust. Let me explain. If the relationship between man and God is that which Christ inaugurated and established, then prayer is no longer a monologue. It is no longer a voice crying in the darkness, but is a real dialogue, and a response not only to a divine precept but also to a promise. 'Pray, and your prayers will be heard.'*
>
> Pope Paul VI, 1897–1978

**Is your prayer life based on using many words, or on a relationship?**

# THE WEDNESDAY OF THE FIRST WEEK IN LENT

*The most famous sign in the world is a 100-metre-long temporary advert for a real estate development. In 1923, the sign 'HOLLYWOODLAND' was erected to advertise a new housing development in the hills above the Hollywood district of Los Angeles. The sign was only meant to be in place for eighteen months, but became synonymous with the golden age of the film industry in LA, and in 1949 was shortened to Hollywood. Today, the sign is so famous it even has its own website.*

*Jonah 3:1–10 The people of Nineveh renounced their evil behaviour*

*Psalm 51:3–4, 12–13, 18–19 A broken and humbled heart, O God, you will not spurn*

*Luke 11:29–32 The only sign given to this generation is the sign of Jonah*

Wherever we go, whatever we do, our lives our governed by signs. 'Stop', 'No Entry', 'Access All Areas', 'Face masks must be worn' – the list of graphic ways of conveying information goes on. I remember a priest once stopped by police for going through a red light. The fact that he was in his late eighties and blind in one eye did not count as mitigating circumstances. In fact, he should not have been driving at all. His (weak) defence was that he had not seen the light.

Some churches like to attract attention with witty signs: 'Life without God is like an unsharpened pencil – no point.' 'Do you spend your time with God's book or Facebook?'

But whether we laugh at witty church signage or obey the 30 mph sign on a deserted country road, signs are important and helpful. They are not simply a means of communication – they demand action. To the people of Nineveh, the sign of Jonah must have seemed a bit odd. Here, in one of the largest cities in the world, the capital of the Neo-Assyrian Empire, was someone wearing sackcloth and ashes, proclaiming imminent doom and gloom. But they responded: 'God saw their efforts to renounce their evil ways. And God relented about the disaster which he said he would bring on them and did not bring it' (Jonah 3:10).

In effect, Lent itself is a sign, and not just that Easter is on the way. It is a sign to us of what Easter is all about: Jesus dying and rising from the dead to give us new life as people of faith. It should not be ignored. It is not the sort of sign to which we can respond 'Sorry, God, but I didn't see it.'

> *Rarely do we realise that we are in the midst of the extraordinary. Miracles occur all around us, signs from God show us the way, angels plead to be heard, but we pay little attention to them because we have been taught that we must follow certain formulas and rules if we want to find God. We do not realise that God is wherever we allow Him/Her to enter.*
>
> Paulo Coelho, Brazilian author, b. 1947

**Do you observe Lent as a sign or simply a penance to be endured?**

# THE THURSDAY OF THE FIRST WEEK IN LENT

The Light of the World *is a painting by the English artist William Holman Hunt (1827–1910). It depicts Christ knocking at a door, waiting to gain entry. The door has no handle and so can only be opened from the inside. 'The closed door', wrote Hunt, 'was the obstinately shut mind.' The painting is in a chapel at Keble College, Oxford.*

*Esther 12:14–16, 23–25 I have no helper but you, Lord*

*Psalm 138:1–3, 7–8 On the day I called you answered me*

*Matthew 7:7–12 Everyone who asks receives*

I suppose I was about seven or eight years old. We were about to go on our summer holidays to the west of Ireland: train from Derby to Crewe, Crewe to Holyhead, the boat to Dun Laoghaire, and then the Westport train from Dublin. I was upstairs getting my clothes ready to go into the big suitcase, to be carried by dad, when suddenly the front door slammed shut. I ran down the stairs crying 'No, no, they've gone without me!' Of course, nobody had gone anywhere. I had not been left alone. To this day, I have no idea why I thought the door slamming signified the end of my summer before it had even begun.

Jesus talks about doors being opened, not closed, and certainly not slammed shut just as you are about to go on your holidays! 'Knock, and the door shall be opened to you … to everyone who knocks the door will be opened' (Matt. 7:7-8). This implies that we have the courage to knock, the courage to ask and, deep down, the firm belief that God hears the person knocking at the door – faith and prayer are based on trust.

Interestingly, Holman Hunt's famous painting depicts Christ himself knocking at the door, wanting to be let in. Crucially, the door has no handle: it can only be opened from the inside. In April 2013, Cardinal Jorge Mario Bergoglio gave a short speech – since dubbed 'The four-minute speech that got Pope Francis elected' – to the cardinals gathered to elect the new pontiff. He referred to the passage in the Book of Revelation which inspired Holman's painting ('Behold I stand at the door and knock,' 3:20). 'But', he said, 'I think about the times in which Jesus knocks from within so that we will let him come out. The self-referential Church keeps Jesus Christ within herself and does not let him out.'

> *How do we pray? Do we pray out of habit, piously but unbothered, or do we put ourselves forward with courage before the Lord to ask for the grace, to ask for what we're praying for? Courage in prayer: a prayer that is not courageous is not a real prayer. The courage to trust that the Lord listens to us, the courage to knock on the door ... The Lord says: 'For everyone who asks, receives; and the one who seeks, finds; and to the one who knocks, the door will be opened.' But you have to ask, seek, and knock.*
>
> Pope Francis, 13 October 2013

**Am I stopping Christ from coming in or from getting out?**

# THE FRIDAY OF THE FIRST WEEK IN LENT

*Lady Justice, a statue by F. W. Pomeroy on top of the Central Criminal Court of England and Wales, popularly known as the Old Bailey. The statue was made in 1905 and 1906, stands sixty metres above the street and is almost four metres high. It is cast in bronze and covered with gold leaf. Lady Justice holds the sword of retribution in her right hand and the equally balanced scales of justice in her left hand.*

*Ezekiel 18:21–28 Would I take pleasure in the death of the wicked and not prefer to see him renounce his wickedness and live?*

*Psalm 130 If you, O Lord, should mark our faults, Lord, who could stand?*

*Matthew 5:20–26 Go and first be reconciled with your brother or sister*

'It wasn't me, Miss – it was him!' A plaintive cry, a heartfelt appeal I suspect has been uttered in many a classroom.

Owning up to even the smallest misdemeanour can be daunting. As children, we would regularly go out and play football on the street in front of the house, where the hedge was just about the right size for the goal. Inevitably, any shot going over the 'bar' would result in the sound of breaking glass followed by a moment's deafening silence and then hasty attempts to apportion blame. In the grand scheme of things, breaking a window does not seem to be a great deal. But it was still hard to own up.

'To err is human; to forgive, divine' is a well-known phrase from a poem written by Alexander Pope in 1711 in his *An Essay on Criticism, Part II*. I am sure the first part applies to every one of us too easily, yet I hope we would all have aspirations toward the second, too.

I have always been struck by the order, or chronology, if you like, of the story recounted by Jesus in Matthew's Gospel: if you are bringing your gift to the altar and remember that someone has a grudge against you, then leave your offering and go and be reconciled. In other words, *you* go and start the reconciliation, even though you may be the innocent party.

As sinners, we seek forgiveness. Pope Francis, who confesses his sins fortnightly in the sacrament of Reconciliation, has said that confession is not about the sins we declare, but the love and healing we receive from God, to go from misery to mercy. As Christians, then, we must not only be forgiving but be the first to take those steps towards reconciliation. The ball is in our court.

> *The first to apologise is the bravest. The first to forgive is the strongest. The first to forget is the happiest.*
> Unknown

**Can you think of a time when you have taken the first step towards reconciliation?**

# THE SATURDAY OF THE FIRST WEEK IN LENT

*Perhaps the most poignant football match ever played was not a major final in a packed stadium but that played between British and German soldiers at what has become known as World War I's Christmas Day truce. On the Western Front on Christmas Eve 1914, British soldiers heard German troops in the trenches opposite them singing carols and saw lanterns shining in their trenches. The soldiers began to shout messages to each other and the next day they met in no man's land, exchanged gifts, took photographs and played football. The* Times *even had a match report on 1 January 1915 about Germany's 3–2 victory. A fibreglass commemorative statue, designed by sculptor Andy Edwards, depicts two figures about to shake hands, capturing the moment the men stopped fighting and played the beautiful game.*

*Deuteronomy 26:16–19 You will be a people holy to the Lord*

*Psalm 119:1–2, 4–5, 7–8 Blessed are those whose way is blameless, who walk in the law of the Lord*

*Matthew 5:43–48 Be perfect as your heavenly Father is perfect*

One of the many memorable scenes in the film *The Godfather, Part II* sees the Corleone family hosting their son's first communion party at Lake Tahoe. During the celebrations, Michael Corleone, Don of the Corleone mafia clan, holds a series of meetings with members of other families. To Frank Pantangeli, once a trusted associate of the Corleone family, he says 'My father taught me many things here – he taught me in this room. He taught me – keep your friends close but your enemies closer.'

Now I am not for one minute suggesting that Jesus inspired the *Godfather* novels and films. Michael Corleone's 'Keep your friends close but your enemies closer' is really about self-protection, being one step ahead of your enemies. But Jesus, of course, lays down a much more radical challenge: 'Love your enemies and pray for those who persecute you' (Matt. 5:44).

The Christmas truce in 1914, a football match between soldiers who remained enemies, has become a symbol of fraternisation. As a student in Rome, I remember in May 1982 attending a special Mass in St Peter's Basilica celebrated by Pope John Paul II for the British and Argentinian communities in Rome. On 2 April, Argentinian forces had invaded and occupied the Falkland Islands, and as the conflict escalated the scheduled papal visit to Great Britain (28 May–2 June) was in doubt. Could the Pope visit a country involved in a military conflict with another? The day before the Mass, Pope John Paul II had lunch with a number of guests, including Cardinal Basil Hume of Westminster, Cardinal Gordon Joseph Gray of St Andrews and Edinburgh, and two Argentinian Cardinals, Raul Primatesta of Cordoba and Juan Carlos de Aramburu of Buenos Aires. Archbishop Thomas Winning of Glasgow, who attended both the lunch and the Mass, said 'The irrationality of the war came home to me as I looked around St Peter's at the young men from South America and Britain. It was just possible that their blood brothers were killing one another in the Falklands at that moment.' The Pope put it bluntly: 'Kill war with words of negotiation rather than kill men with the sword.'

---

*Loving your enemies. Far from being the pious injunction of a utopian dreamer, this demand is an absolute necessity for the survival of our civilisation. Yes, it is love that will save our world and civilisation; love even for our enemies.*

Martin Luther King Jr., 1929–1968

---

**Jesus says if we only greet our friends, we are not doing anything exceptional. Can you reach out to those who are not your best friends?**

# The Second Week of Lent

# THE SUNDAY OF THE SECOND WEEK IN LENT

*The majority of station clocks are based on the 1944 Swiss design by Hans Hilfiker. In 1953 he added a red second hand to its design in the shape of a railway guard's signalling disc. The clock owes its technology to the particular requirements of operating a railway: timetables do not list seconds and trains always leave the station on the full minute. The station clocks in Switzerland are synchronised by receiving an electrical impulse from a central master clock at each full minute, advancing the hand. The second hand is driven by an electrical motor independent of the master clock.*

*Genesis 15:5–12, 17–18 God enters into a Covenant with Abraham, the man of faith*

*Psalm 27:1, 7–9, 13–14 The Lord is my light and my salvation*

*Philippians 3:17 – 4:1 Christ will transform this wretched body of ours into the mould of his glorious body*

*Luke 9:28–36 As Jesus prayed, the aspect of his face was changed*

Certainty can be comforting, providing a degree of safety and security. The certainty of trains being on time, running like clockwork, is, some might say, an aspiration in the United Kingdom. In Switzerland, trains are renowned for punctuality and reliability. Twenty years ago, a British journalist said 'It is a system to be admired. The trains really do run like clockwork; they are seldom late and when you need to make a connection it is often waiting for you on the next platform. Just before Christmas I heard a Swiss train had been cancelled for the first time in 100 years due to lack of drivers.'

My dad would never get on a train without first asking station staff if it was the one he needed. In the meanwhile, his impatient children were clambering aboard, having assured him that it already been announced as the right one. Mum always smiled at us all. The first time she caught a train after dad died, she dispensed with the need to check with the station staff. A few minutes later, the train pulled out of the station in the opposite direction from the one she wanted. I am sure dad was watching, laughing away!

In the Book of Genesis Abram is promised a great land, but needs some assurance: 'Lord God, how can I know that I shall possess it?' (15:8). Abram is called to place his trust in the Lord. In the account of the Transfiguration Peter, James and John are asked to do likewise: 'This is my Son, the Chosen One. Listen to him' (Luke 9:35).

Lent is a time to stop and listen to the voice of the Lord, the voice that calls us to conversion. If we listen to his words, if we imitate his actions, then perhaps we, too, will hear God say to us 'You are my child, the beloved.'

---

*In meditating on this passage of the Gospel, we can learn a very important lesson from it: first of all, the primacy of prayer, without which the entire commitment to the apostolate and to charity is reduced to activism. In Lent we learn to give the right time to prayer, both personal and of the community, which gives breath to our spiritual life. Moreover, prayer does not mean isolating oneself from the world and from its contradictions, as Peter wanted to do on Mount Tabor; rather, prayer leads back to the journey and to action. 'The Christian life', I wrote in my Message for this Lent, 'consists in continuously scaling the mountain to meet God and then coming back down, bearing the love and strength drawn from him, so as to serve our brothers and sisters with God's own love'.*

Pope Benedict XVI, 24 February 2013

---

**'Listen to him.' How do I allow God's voice to be heard in the busy-ness of daily life?**

# THE MONDAY OF THE SECOND WEEK IN LENT

*The Coat of Arms of Pope Francis, with the Latin motto 'miserando atque eligendo' – 'By showing compassion and by choosing'. At the top of the shield is the official seal of the Society of Jesus, representing Jesus and the religious order in which the Pope was ordained in 1969. The symbol shows a blazing yellow sun with the red letters IHS, the first three letters of the Latinised transcription of the Greek name for Jesus. A red cross rises up from the letter H and three black nails rest below. Beneath, to the left, is the eight-pointed star, which, according to heraldic tradition, is a symbol of Our Lady, mother of Christ and of the Church; to the right, a spikenard flower, which in Spanish iconography symbolises Saint Joseph. Spikenard or nard produces a costly aromatic ointment (cf. Mark 14:3 and John 12:3).*

*Daniel 9:4–10 We have sinned, we have done wrong*

*Psalm 79:8–9, 11, 13 Do not treat us according to our sins, O Lord*

*Luke 6:36–38 Forgive, and you will be forgiven*

Many organisations will boast about their key values, their mission statement, purpose, vision, maybe even their outreach programme. You can probably find websites that construct many of these for you, listing the appropriate and attractive nouns, verbs and adjectives. Some schools, too, may have coats of arms and centuries-old mottos, usually in Latin, proclaiming the school's USP (unique selling point or proposition). A well-known multinational conglomerate corporation specialising in electronic goods such as TVs, computer games and so on stated that its aim was 'to be a company that inspires and fulfils your curiosity', while a fast-food company declares its purpose 'to feed and foster communities'. Or how about the company whose mission is to be 'one of the world's leading producers and providers of entertainment and information, using its portfolio of brands to differentiate its content, services and consumer products'? And I thought Disney was all about cartoons and films! Nowadays, even trendier than mission statements is the 'elevator pitch' – a brief, persuasive speech, lasting no longer than twenty or thirty seconds, which describes and arouses interest in whatever an organisation does.

In our modern world of mission and vision statements, key values and outreach, it is easy to lose sight of the very basic message Jesus puts before us. Here is a mission for us all. It sets out values which should characterise our lives as

Christians: be compassionate, do not judge, do not condemn, grant pardon, and give, because the amount you measure out is the amount you will be given back.

If you were accused of being a Christian, would there be enough evidence to convict you? Would the prosecution case be based on your obvious compassion and forgiveness of others, a life characterised by giving rather than taking? Or, to put it another way, if your baptismal records were lost, what evidence would you give at the gates of heaven to demonstrate you had strived to lead a Christian life?

> *Delivering value to the client, meeting their needs and, wherever possible, exceeding their expectations, is to fulfil the golden rule to 'love your neighbour as yourself' (Matt. 23:29). In serving and loving others we are serving God inasmuch as humanity bears the imago Dei.*
>
> *Whatever institution we work in, whether it be commercial, ecclesiastical, profit or non-profit driven, its godly purpose is to deliver value. The gospel, whether worked out in the marketplace or the church, is about articulating this.*
>
> Bill Westwood, 'The Marketing Value Proposition',
> *Faith in Business Quarterly*

**If you had twenty or thirty seconds to describe what you do to further mission of the Church, what would you say?**

# The Tuesday of the Second Week in Lent

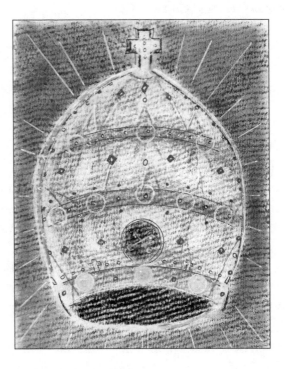

*The papal tiara is a crown worn by popes of the Catholic Church until 1963.*

*From 1143 to 1963 at the papal coronation the new Pope was crowned with a tiara. In 1964, Pope Paul VI descended the steps of the papal throne in St Peter's Basilica and ascended to the altar on which he laid the tiara as a sign of the renunciation of human glory and power in keeping with the renewed spirit of the Second Vatican Council. It was announced that the tiara would be sold and the money given to charity. It was bought by Catholics in the United States and is now kept in the Basilica of the National Shrine of the Immaculate Conception in Washington, DC.*

*Isaiah 1:10, 16–20 Learn to do good, search for justice*

*Psalm 50:8–9, 16–17, 21, 23 To one who is blameless I will show the salvation of God*

*Matthew 23:1–12 They do not practice what they preach*

I remember accompanying a priest to the Roman shop Ditta Annibale Gammarelli, where the papal robes are made. As its website proudly declared, 'For over two hundred years the famous Gammarelli family have been at the heart of serving the clergy. From deacons to Popes everyone experiences the same courtesy and attention to detail. There is an old saying, "you get what you pay for", [and] this is certainly true here. Quality is at the heart of the service offered by the Gammarelli family.'

The priest had been appointed a monsignor and wanted to buy the necessary monsignorial robes. The first question was 'What type of monsignor?' My priest friend looked perplexed. Signor Gammarelli patiently explained the three different ranks of monsignor (reduced from fourteen, thankfully!) – Protonotary Apostolic, Honorary Prelate and, finally, Chaplain of His Holiness – and the specific dress requirements for each, which include the number of purple buttons on a cassock (in the Roman Catholic Church there are thirty-three buttons to represent the years of Jesus' life). You can imagine the horror, or the tearing of purple watered silk sashes, in some circles when, shortly after his election, Pope Francis abolished the practice of granting priests under the age of sixty-five the title of monsignor.

Status and important titles mean nothing if they are not backed up by Jesus' simple admonition to practise what you preach. This challenge is laid down for every Christian, indeed every human being, and not just those with thirty-three buttons on a purple cassock.

> *Power is also fleeting, here today, gone tomorrow ... It is important if you can do good with power. Jesus defined power: true power is service, serving others, serving the poor. And I still have to advance on this path of service, because I feel that I don't do everything I must do. That is how I feel about power.*
> Pope Francis, 27 September 2015

**How is what you profess in faith actively expressed in your family life, relationships and work?**

# THE WEDNESDAY OF THE SECOND WEEK IN LENT

*Commander of the Order of the British Empire (CBE) is the highest-ranking Order of the British Empire. King George V created the awards during World War I to reward services to the war effort by people helping back within the United Kingdom, those not on the front line.*

*Jeremiah 18:18–20 Come on, let us slander him*

*Psalm 31:5–6, 14–16 Save me in your merciful love, O Lord*

*Matthew 20:17–28 They will condemn him to death*

Whenever the New Year's Honours List is published I always say, perhaps forlornly, 'Well, looks like I've been missed out again!' I suspect everyone likes their just rewards. I do not mean this in a negative sense. Good work should equal meaningful rewards.

At a very young and impressionable age, we were told about Santa's 'naughty and nice' list. If your deeds throughout the year meant your name appeared in the former, then Santa would leave coal in your Christmas stocking. If you made it on to the latter, sweets would be the reward.

In its 2020 Christmas advert, a well-known supermarket, conscious of the morale of the nation in the midst of a pandemic, had customers make their own naughty confessions: 'I may have bought too many loo rolls.' 'I once forgot to sing "Happy birthday" when I washed my hands.' Even Santa said 'I might have gone on holiday.' 'But relax!' the voiceover declared. 'After *this* year, there is no "naughty list". You have all the treats you want.' So everybody gets whatever they want; everyone is rewarded.

Pope Francis once remarked that there are lots of climbers in the Church and suggested it might be better for them 'to go north and become mountain climbers! It's healthier. But don't come to Church to climb!' In Matthew's Gospel, the mother of Zebedee's sons wants to see them suitably rewarded, presumably for their following of Jesus. Here is a natural, maternal instinct – to see her children do well, in this case by getting the best seats in heaven. But one of the characteristics of following Jesus is that many of the world's values are simply turned on their heads. 'Anyone who wants to become great among you must be your servant, and anyone who wants to be first among you must be your servant' (Matt. 20:26–27).

> *When the end comes, you will be esteemed by the world and rewarded by God, not because you have won the love and respect of the princes of the earth, however powerful, but rather for having loved, defended and cherished one such as I ... what you receive from others is a testimony to their virtue; but all that you do for others is the sign and clear indication of your own.*
>
> Giordano Bruno, Italian friar,
> philosopher and polymath, 1548–1600

**Where and how do you really look for rewards?**

# THE THURSDAY OF THE SECOND WEEK IN LENT

*Italian sculptor Lorenzo Quinn is well known for his representations of human hands. 'I wanted to sculpt what is considered the hardest and most technically challenging part of the human body. The hand holds so much power – the power to love, to hate, to create, to destroy.' 'Trust' is a sculpture of a male hand gently supporting a female figure. Quinn comments: 'The most wonderful feeling and greatest responsibility is that of knowing that someone has complete trust in you. That feeling of total unabated abandonment in your hands.'*

*Jeremiah 17:5–10 Cursed be anyone who trusts in human beings, who relies on human strength, blessed is anyone who trusts in the Lord*

*Psalm 1:1–4, 6 Blessed the one who has placed all trust in the Lord*

*Luke 16:19–31 During your life you had your fill of good things, just as Lazarus his fill of bad. Now he is being comforted here while you are in agony*

Team building is often a key component of executive away-days designed to set strategy and assess the direction of travel (and whatever other jargon springs to mind!). One of the most well-known team building exercises involves the blindfolding of an individual who is then asked to fall backwards, trusting that colleagues will catch him or her, preventing a crash to the floor. Here is a simple act of trust that prevents one coming to harm.

According to UK polls, nurses are the most trusted professionals in Britain. It also seems there may be some truth in the admonition 'Trust me, I'm a doctor.' The least-trusted professionals are politicians, followed by advertising executives. Also close to the bottom of the trust table are journalists and estate agents, while for clergy the trust stakes have been on a downward trajectory for some years.

'Blessed the one who has placed all trust in the Lord' (Ps. 40:5); 'Cursed be anyone who trusts in human beings, who relies on human strength' (Jer. 17:5). The invitation to put one's trust in God is not an 'if-all-else-fails' invitation, but a foundational one: to trust in God from the outset, so that, as the prophet Jeremiah suggests, using the wonderful image of a tree by the waterside, 'untroubled in a year of drought, it never stops bearing fruit' (17:8).

Drought, the sense that God is not listening or that prayer is an arid experience, will come to all of us: that is the real challenge of trust. The Spanish mystic and poet St John of the Cross (1542–1591) called it the 'Dark Night of the Soul' while the letters of St Teresa of Calcutta suggest she may have experienced such spiritual dryness from 1947 until just before her death in 1997. She had a deep sense of God's absence: 'In my soul', she wrote, 'I feel just that terrible pain of loss – of God not wanting me – of God not being God – of God not really existing.' At times of drought, the easy answer is to seek nourishment and solace elsewhere; the words of the Psalm call on us to remain beside the flowing waters, so that everything we do shall prosper.

> *God does not demand that I be successful. God demands that I be faithful. When facing God, results are not important. Faithfulness is what is important.*
> St Teresa of Calcutta, 1910–1997

**Have you experienced that spiritual drought of St Teresa of Calcutta, and at such times how challenging is it to place your trust in God?**

# THE FRIDAY OF THE SECOND WEEK IN LENT

Joseph and the Amazing Technicolor Dreamcoat *was first performed in 1968 as a fifteen-minute show in a London school before the full spectacle opened in London's West End in 1973. The show has no spoken dialogue and is completely sung. In September 1991, with Jason Donovan in the lead role, the soundtrack topped the UK album charts, with over one million sales. The coat worn in a recent production spanned 12 metres, weighed 20 kilograms and cost £10,000.*

*Genesis 37:3–4, 12–13, 17b–28 Here comes that dreamer. Come on, let us kill him*

*Psalm 105:16–21 Remember the wonders the Lord has done*

*Matthew 21:33–43, 45–46 This is the heir. Come on, let us kill him*

Tim Rice and Andrew Lloyd Webber are famous for a string of musical productions, some (but not all) co-written – *Jesus Christ Superstar, Cats, Phantom of the Opera* and *The Lion King* to name but a few. But the first Lloyd Webber–Rice musical to be performed publicly was *Joseph and the Amazing Technicolor Dreamcoat*, and the cast of those who have played the title role reads like a list of pop idols of the last half century: David Cassidy, Jason Donovan, Donny Osmond, Phillip Schofield, Stephen Gately and many more.

I remember seeing the production a number of times at Derby Playhouse in the 1970s. The venue did not quite attract the pop stars of the day, but that did not detract from the quality of the performances. Of course, I was watching a fun musical in the days before I had any real awareness of the complexities of the real biblical narrative and the theatrical licence taken by Lloyd Webber and Rice: Joseph had a coat of long sleeves, not a technicolor dreamcoat; in the biblical text, Judah says to his brothers 'Come, let us sell him to the Ishmaelites …' while the next paragraph begins 'Now some Midianite merchants were passing, and they pulled Joseph out of the well. They sold Joseph to the Ishmaelites for twenty shekels of silver, and these took Joseph to Egypt' (Gen. 37:28). The musical was not quite so confusing!

At the heart of the Old Testament narrative is jealousy.

Joseph's brothers do not like their dreamer sibling, and so they get rid of him, just like the tenants in the parable in Matthew's Gospel who kill the son in order to take his inheritance. Shakespeare provided us with the memorable image of jealousy in his 'green-ey'd monster' (*Othello*, Act 3, Scene 1) and it is a fact that jealousy can drive people to monstrous acts. But God's way is different: 'The stone that the builders rejected has become the cornerstone' (Ps. 118:22). We must learn to see, judge and act with God's eyes, not through the lens of a green-eyed monster.

> *Anger, passion, ignorance, prejudice, greed, envy, covetousness, jealousy and suspicion prevent man from ascending to the realms of holiness, imprisoning him in the claws of self and the cage of egotism.*
>
> 'Abdu'l-Bahá, 1844–1921,
> head of the Bahá'í Faith 1892–1921

**Envy or jealousy is termed one of the 'seven deadly sins.' Do you think this is excessive? How harmful do you think it can really be?**

# THE SATURDAY OF THE SECOND WEEK IN LENT

The Return of the Prodigal Son *by Rembrandt van Rijn (1606–1669) is housed in the Hermitage Museum in St Petersburg and was described by art critic Kenneth Clark as 'a picture which those who have seen the original in St Petersburg may be forgiven for claiming as the greatest picture ever painted'.*

*Micah 7:14–15, 18–20 Tread down our faults; throw all our sins to the bottom of the sea*

*Psalm 103:1–4, 9–12 The Lord is compassionate and gracious*

*Luke 15:1–3, 11–32 Your brother here was dead and has come to life*

As a sport-mad child, I loved watching and playing almost any kind of game. But only once did I play rugby: as I held the rugby ball, wondering what to do next, other players at least twice my size and build came running towards me – so I gave it to them! Strangely enough, that was the last time I was picked for the team.

On TV, I loved watching *A Question of Sport*, which began in January 1970, presented by David Vine with teams captained by Henry Cooper and Cliff Morgan. My favourite round of the quiz was 'What happened next?' in which footage from a sporting occasion was shown and stopped mid-action, leaving the teams to try and guess … well, what happened next. I would not dare to say I was good at it, but it was great fun.

In the well-known story of the prodigal son, the focus can be on the loving, merciful father, or on the son who comes to his senses and returns home, or on the elder son who refuses to join the party.

The father explains: 'My son, you are with me always and all I have is yours. But it was only right we should celebrate and rejoice, because your brother here was dead and has come to life; he was lost and is found' (Luke 15:32). The gospel account ends here. But, I wonder, what happened next? Of course, I know this is a parable recounted by Jesus and there is no factual answer. Sometimes, we hear about people being in the last-chance saloon, but the image of God the Father portrayed by Jesus is not that of a bouncer outside the club doors. God does not compare the two sons to see who comes top of the table: he loves them both, equally, all the time. The same not only applies to us, but also lays down a challenge to us to love in the same way. So, what will happen next?

> *The fatted calf, the best Scotch, the hoedown could all have been his, too, any time he asked for them, except that he never thought to ask for them because he was too busy trying cheerlessly and religiously to earn them.*
> Frederick Buechner, American theologian b. 1926

**Think of a situation in your own life and how you approach it as the father, the prodigal son and the elder son. What would you do next?**

# THE THIRD WEEK
## OF LENT

# THE SUNDAY OF THE THIRD WEEK IN LENT

*Statue of Leonardo da Vinci (1452–1519) in Milan's Piazza della Scala. The statue is the work of Pietro Magni (1872). While in Milan, Leonardo designed the system to make the city's canals travelable and navigation from Lake Como to Milan possible. A plaque on the statue reads 'Guest long-envied in Milan, where he had friends – disciples – glory.'*

*Exodus 3:1-8, 13-15 I Am has sent me to you*

*Psalm 103:1-4, 6-8 The Lord is compassionate and gracious*

*1 Corinthians 10:1-6, 10-12 The life of the people under Moses in the desert was written down to instruct us*

*Luke 13:1-9 Unless you repent you will all perish as they did*

I wonder how many times you have heard the phrase 'It'll look good on your CV.' Here is a major growth industry where professional experts abound, telling you what to include in your personal profile, and how to state what you can bring to the table and highlight your key achievements. Genuine examples of the latter include such gems as 'I've won a variety of eating competitions across the world', 'I came first in the (primary) school long-distance race' and 'I forced myself to like olives.' While all these unique achievements reveal something about the person behind the resumé, they may not be those desired or necessary for that high-profile executive role.

What is believed to be the oldest CV in the world was in fact sent in 1481 or 1482 by Leonardo da Vinci to a potential employer, Ludovico Sforza. Da Vinci begins: 'Most illustrious Lord, having now sufficiently seen and considered the proofs of all those who count themselves master and inventors of instruments of war, and finding that their invention and use of the said instruments does not differ in any respect from those in common practice, I am emboldened without prejudice to anyone else to put myself in communication with your Excellency, in order to acquaint you with my secrets, thereafter offering myself at your pleasure effectually to demonstrate at any convenient time all those matters which are in part briefly recorded below …' He then provides a ten-point summary of his skills as a military engineer (just what Sforza was looking for) before ending 'Also I can execute sculpture in marble, bronze and clay. Likewise in painting, I can do everything possible as well as any other, whosoever he may be.' Nice to know that this skilled engineer could also produce works like the marble statue of David in Florence and the painting of the Last Judgement in the Sistine Chapel!

Perhaps in an attempt to make faith and religion cool and trendy, there have been occasions when people have drafted a CV for Jesus, who is applying 'for the top executive position in your heart'. Listed qualifications include creation of heaven and earth; skills and work experience include helping the poor, healing the sick and curing people from physical ailments. And, of course, references could be sought from followers throughout the world.

For a list of what the Lord brings to us, look no further than Psalm 103: 'The Lord is compassionate and gracious' (v. 8). My guilt is forgiven by the Lord, my ills healed, the Lord 'redeems [my] life from the pit' (v. 3). Psalm 103 is about the difference the Lord can make to our own lives, if we allow him to come into them, or, in modern parlance I suppose, accept 'his CV' as the one that will make a difference: 'The Lord is compassionate and gracious, slow to anger and rich in mercy … For as the heavens are high above the earth, so strong is his mercy for those who fear him' (vv. 8, 11).

*Compassion allows you to see reality; compassion is like the lens of the heart: it allows us to take in and understand the true dimensions. In the Gospels, Jesus is often moved by compassion. And compassion is also the language of God. Our God is a God of compassion, and compassion – we can say – is the weakness of God, but also his strength. If compassion is the language of God, so often human language is that of indifference. We must ask ourselves: 'How many times do we look away?' By doing so we close the door to compassion. We must make an examination of conscience: Do I usually look the other way? Or do I allow the Holy Spirit to place me on the path of compassion?*

Pope Francis, 17 September 2019

**As a believer and person of faith, what would you put on your CV?**

# THE MONDAY OF THE THIRD WEEK IN LENT

*Rome's Basilica of San Lorenzo in Lucina is dedicated to St Laurence and the original church dates back to the middle of the fifth century. The church was rebuilt in the twelfth century and relics of saints were collected as part of the project. A side chapel is dedicated to St Laurence and beneath the altar is a bronze grille through which can be seen a reliquary containing part of the gridiron used in his martyrdom.*

*2 Kings 5:1-15 There were many lepers in Israel, but none of these was cured, except the Syrian, Naaman*

*Psalm 42:2-3; 43:3-4 My soul is thirsting for God, the living God; when can I enter and appear before the face of God?*

*Luke 4:24-30 Like Elijah and Elisha, Jesus is not sent to the Jews only*

Romans love St Laurence. There are thirty-one churches dedicated to him throughout the city, making him second only to Christ, Mary, St John the Baptist and St Peter in terms of devotion. St Laurence was a deacon in Rome during the reign of Pope Sixtus II. In August 258, the Emperor Valerian issued an edict that all bishops, priests and deacons be put to death. Pope Sixtus II and six deacons were beheaded, leaving Laurence as the senior church official. Four days later, Laurence was summoned to appear before the Prefect of Rome and told to bring the treasures of the Church with him. He arrived accompanied by beggars, the sick and the crippled – those who survived on his charity. 'These', Laurence said, 'are the treasures of the Church.' For such insolence, he was sentenced to death by grilling over a slow fire. After suffering a long time, he said with a cheerful smile 'Turn me over – one side is done.' The Prefect of Rome ordered this to be done, whereupon Laurence invited him to test whether he tasted better cooked or raw. Then, having prayed for the conversion of Rome that the faith of Christ might spread from there throughout the world, Laurence died.

The Prefect of Rome really only wanted one answer to his question about the riches of the Church. He wanted its material wealth. Unexpected answers, unexpected situations, present a challenge. 'You come out of a crisis', a priest friend once said, 'better or bitter.'

Naaman, the army commander suffering from leprosy, seems to be expecting at the very least some dramatic healing or personal divine intervention to justify his budget of ten talents of silver, six thousand shekels of gold and ten festal robes. The people of Nazara in the Gospel were expecting a Messiah with a bit of a more glorious background than that of their own sleepy little village.

How easy it is for all of us to set the parameters into which God must fit, and to be bemused, if not indignant, if God dares to reveal himself in some other way. The word of God expressed through Elisha, Elijah, Laurence and the many other witnesses does not provide us with a sense of entitlement. Should we get to the pearly gates, our opening line should not be 'Don't you know who I am?' but 'My soul is thirsting for God, the living God; when can I enter and appear before the face of God?' (Ps. 42:3).

*We live in a consumer driven culture, and because we do, most of the time we bring a preconceived notion to a given situation that we deserve more. We deserve better. We deserve something different than what is presented before us, whether it means a lane of traffic all to ourselves, an unbroken travel schedule, or regular promotions at the office.*

*And that's really the thing at the heart of all our entitlement issues, isn't it? Isn't it whether we really trust the Lord to give us what we need? Isn't it whether we really believe He is good enough and wise enough to provide? And isn't that when we feel so entitled to something more than what we are experiencing that we are actually calling into question the very wisdom and power of God on our behalf?*

*What do we all do when we feel the impulse inside of us that says we deserve more and better? We trust. Again and again. And when we do, we fix our eyes on Jesus, who knew full well what He was entitled to, and yet laid it all down because He trusted the wisdom, timing, and power of the Father.*

Michael Kelley, 'Faith is the Escape Hatch for Entitlement', online article

**Which characteristic is more fundamental to faith: entitlement or humility?**

# THE TUESDAY OF THE THIRD WEEK IN LENT

*The Busicom LE-120A, known as the Handy, was one of the first hand-held calculators small enough to really be described as 'pocket-sized'. It was manufactured by the Japanese Nippon Calculating Machine Corporation, which later changed its name to Busicom Corp (Business Computer Corporation). The Handy went on sale in January 1971 at a cost of around £165. Since it was so expensive, it came with a wrist strap attached at its base to protect it from being dropped. Aristotle Onassis, the Greek shipping magnate, used to give them as gifts to friends.*

*Daniel 3:25, 34–43 In contrition of heart and humility of spirit may we be acceptable to you*

*Psalm 25:4–9 Remember your compassion, O Lord*

*Matthew 18:21–35 Your Father will not forgive you unless you each forgive your brother and sister from your heart*

I passed Mathematics O level at the end of the Fourth Form (such phrases are beginning to show my age!) and studied Mathematics A level … for a fortnight. I struggled with all those numbers, and, perhaps more importantly in my sport-obsessed mind, Maths clashed with football practice. There was only ever going to be one winner. To be honest, numbers never were my strong point, although I do remember the hours of fun we had trying to spell words on our calculators: in the block Roman script, 43770 spelt 'HELLO'. Such fun!

The apostle Peter seems concerned about numbers: 'Lord, how often must I forgive my brother or sister who wrongs me? As often as seven times?' (Matt. 18:21). I suspect it is all too easy to side with Peter's logical approach, ensuring you are doing the right thing but wondering how far you have to go.

Where true forgiveness is concerned, numbers are irrelevant – that is the challenge laid down by Jesus. It lies not in numerical certainty, but in true forgiveness from the heart. Forgiveness is not an intellectual exercise like learning times tables or fractions, or even the precise value of pi to all its current 62.8 trillion decimal places. Forgiveness is an act of love to all those who have done wrong. And true forgiveness is infinite.

*How much suffering, how many wounds, how many wars could be avoided if forgiveness and mercy were the style of our life! Even in families, even in families. How many disunited families, who do not know how to forgive each other. How many brothers and sisters bear this resentment within. It is necessary to apply merciful love to all human relationships: between spouses, between parents and children, within our communities, in the Church and also in society and politics.*

*Today's parable helps us to grasp fully the meaning of that phrase we recite in the Lord's Prayer: 'And forgive us our trespasses, as we forgive those who trespass against us' (cf. Matt. 6:12). These words contain a decisive truth. We cannot demand God's forgiveness for ourselves if we in turn do not grant forgiveness to our neighbour. It is a condition: think of your end, of God's forgiveness, and stop hating. Reject resentment, that bothersome fly that keeps coming back. If we do not strive to forgive and to love, we will not be forgiven and loved either.*

Pope Francis, 13 September 2020

**Do you forgive from the heart or the head?**

# THE WEDNESDAY OF THE THIRD WEEK IN LENT

*The most expensive burger in the world is the FleurBurger 5000 from the Fleur de Lys in Mandalay Bay in Las Vegas, Nevada. It costs $5,000 (fries included). The burger is made of wagyu beef and there is accompanying foie gras and a truffle sauce, all served on a brioche truffle bun with black truffles on the side. It comes with a bottle of 1995 Chateau Petrus, valued at $2,500.*

*Deuteronomy 4:1, 5–9 Listen to the laws and observe them*

*Psalm 147:12–13, 15–16, 19–20 O Jerusalem, glorify the Lord!*

*Matthew 5:17–19 Anyone who keeps these commandments and teaches them will be called great in the kingdom of Heaven*

Many, many years ago, the Sunday magazine of a national newspaper used to feature collections of factual, fictional and humorous lists subsequently published as the *Book of JournoLISTS*. They included 'Ten signs that you have made it as a soccer star' and 'Ten things to do before going to a "nouvelle cuisine" restaurant' (where one piece of advice was 'Have a decent meal before you go'). Of course, this is many years before cookery programmes were commonplace on the weekly TV menu and words and phrases like 'on a *jus* of…' and '*amuse-bouche*' were largely unknown. Now, we are quite used to set and *à la carte* menus, choosing what we want and ignoring the rest.

There is a temptation to see faith in the same way – to believe in the bits we like (or at worst are the most comfortable) and ignore the rest. 'And now, Israel, listen to the laws and customs that I am teaching you [and observe them],' says Moses in the Book of Deuteronomy (4:1). Jesus echoes this: 'Anyone who infringes even one of the least of these commandments and teaches others to do the same will be called least in the kingdom of Heaven; but anyone who keeps them and teaches them will be called great in the kingdom of Heaven' (Matt. 5:19).

Today, there is a great temptation to relegate religion and

belief to the private sphere, perhaps as an *à la carte* aspect of today's society. You do not have to choose them, but they are there if you want them. If we claim to be Christian, though, there are no such options. I cannot be a Sunday-only Christian. Christians are called to a life founded on and nourished by a relationship with God, a relationship which informs the way we live, the way we speak and the way we act, and the daily choices we make.

> *There is no question, too, of becoming Catholics by accepting our teaching à la carte. We have to take the menu or go to another restaurant.*
> Cardinal George Basil Hume, 1923–1999

**Is faith and practice of faith *à la carte*?**

# THE THURSDAY OF THE THIRD WEEK IN LENT

*As a Christmas gift in December 2020 Pope Francis gave each of the Vatican employees five packs of a paracetamol-based flu remedy. 'Pope Francis gives Vatican employees flu medicine for Christmas' was one headline, while another declared 'Long live reality and health. That's the Pope's gift. How beautiful.'*

*Jeremiah 7:23–28 This is the nation that will neither listen to the voice of the Lord its God nor take correction*

*Psalm 95:1–2, 6–9 O that today you would listen to his voice! 'Harden not your hearts'*

*Luke 11:14–23 Anyone who is not with me is against me*

When I worked in the Vatican, all employees received a Christmas gift from the Pope: a bottle of Prosecco and panettone (rich, fruity, sweet bread, often eaten at Christmas – Italian Christmas cake!). It was a nice, simple gesture. At Vatican Radio, the gifts would be handed out to staff by the director. Times change. In 2020, Pope Francis gave employees five packs of Vicks flu remedy. Whether the gift was to ward off any impending hangovers or just an infallible papal antidote for flu, who knows.

Christmas in the Vatican has been headline news in recent years due to what has been perceived as Pope Francis' stinging criticisms of his own bureaucracy, the Roman curia, when they gather for the traditional exchange of Christmas greetings. In 2014, newspapers reported how the cardinals sat stony-faced as the Pope listed their fifteen ailments, including a feeling of being indispensable, a terrorism of gossip, careerism and opportunism. 'The prelates politely, but unenthusiastically, applauded at the end,' said one newspaper.

In 2020, the Pope spoke about the damage caused by division in the Church. Of course, this is nothing new. 'Every kingdom divided against itself is heading for ruin, and a household divided against itself collapses,' says Jesus (Luke 14:17). The prophet Jeremiah paints an equally sombre picture of those who refused to listen to God's voice: 'But they did not listen, they did not pay attention; they followed their own devices, their own stubborn and wicked inclinations, and got worse rather than better' (7:24).

It is perhaps ironic that today the phrase commonly used to signify a sense of unity – 'singing from the same hymn sheet' – has a religious connotation (although some years ago a district council did ask officials to stop using the phrase to avoid upsetting non-believers). Religious belief and practice is not about taking sides and ensuring you come out on top. It is about echoing and manifesting in our daily lives the words of the Psalmist: 'O come; let us bow and bend low. Let us kneel before the God who made us, for he is our God and we the people who belong to his pasture, the flock that is led by his hand' (Ps. 95:6–7).

> *When the Church is viewed in terms of conflict – right versus left, progressive versus traditionalist – she becomes fragmented and polarised, distorting and betraying her true nature. She is, on the other hand, a body in continual crisis, precisely because she is alive. She must never become a body in conflict, with winners and losers, for in this way she would spread apprehension, become more rigid and less synodal, and impose a uniformity far removed from the richness and plurality that the Spirit has bestowed on his Church.*
>
> Pope Francis, 21 December 2020

**What harm can be caused by division in your parish and community and how can it be healed?**

# The Friday of the Third Week in Lent

*The TV quiz show* Mastermind *began in 1972 and its Soft Pad lounge chair was designed by Charles and Ray Eames. It is considered by some to be the real star of the show.*

*In 1979, the chair was kidnapped, and a £50 ransom demanded by students at the University of Ulster for their Cambodia Relief Fund. In 2009, the chair was voted the second most iconic chair of the twentieth century. Today, such a chair would cost nearly £4,000.*

*Hosea 14:2–10 We will not say any more 'Our God' to the work of our own hands*

*Psalm 81:6, 8–11, 14, 17 I am the Lord your God; listen as I warn you*

*Mark 12:28–34 The Lord our God is the one Lord, and you must love him*

Quiz shows are part of the staple diet of television schedules. The different formats cater for different audiences throughout the day, from the afternoon entertainment quiz shows when you sometimes think the focus is really on the contestant or team rather than on the quiz itself, to the more challenging, academic quizzes in the later evening. Quiz shows demonstrate both our thirst for entertainment and for knowledge, even though I sometimes hope I might get a point just for understanding the question, never mind being able to answer it!

The need to answer questions does not just concern entertainment. From primary school SATs through to GCSEs, A levels and beyond, it is as if we are being tested all our lives. And who knows at what level the pass mark might be set.

It is an examination-type question which is put to Jesus by one of the Scribes, an expert in law, although not necessarily one opposed to Jesus: 'Which is the first of all the commandments?' (Mark 12:28). Jesus does not 'pass' on this enquiry, as we see happening in so many quizzes today: the first commandment is that there is one God and no other, and the second is to love your neighbour as yourself.

If this were a tick-box questionnaire, the matter would end here, and it would be on to the next set of questions.

But the challenge of being a Christian is not about picking options on a form. It is about living out the example given by Jesus in daily life.

> *Jesus summed up the law as loving God with all your heart, with all your soul and with all your strength; love also your neighbour as yourself. Judged by God's ideal I am chief sinner of all. However, I am amazed and renewed by God's forgiveness which is his miracle in me. My path is open to God because Jesus Christ, who was without sin, died for my disconnectedness with God. He has set me free. I am forgiven. There is nothing I can do to make God love me less. That is the amazing nature of grace.*
>
> Archbishop John Sentamu,
> Archbishop of York 2005–2020

**'Mind the gap': can this be applied to a tick-box and lived approach to faith and witness?**

# THE SATURDAY OF THE THIRD WEEK IN LENT

*During his 2010 visit to the UK, Pope Benedict XVI travelled around in a modified Mercedes-Benz M Class sport utility vehicle known as the Popemobile. The white car has bulletproof glass, reinforced armoured side panels and undercarriage, a hydraulic seat, and is designed with a glass enclosure, which means the Pope can be seen when travelling through large crowds. The vehicle has room for the Pope, two aides, a security guard and the driver. For security reasons, its top speed was not revealed ('it goes as fast as it needs to go'), but the average speed during the trip was six miles per hour.*

*Hosea 5:15 – 6:6 My pleasure is in faithful love, not sacrifice*

*Psalm 50:3–4, 18–21 What I want is faithful love, not sacrifice*

*Luke 18:9–14 The tax collector went home again justified; the Pharisee did not*

For me, a car is a means of getting from A to B. I do not have to make any really long journeys, but I want a car which is reliable and efficient. Sales talk about the particular trim, dashboard accessories and so on does not interest me, even less the whole question of personalised registrations. Vatican cars bear the number plates 'SCV 1', 'SCV 2' and so on, SCV being the acronym for *Stato della Città del Vaticano* – Vatican City State – or, as we used to say, '*Se Cristo videsse*' ('If only Christ could see it now!').

Personalised plates are sometimes a sign of status – 'Look at me!' – and there is something profoundly human about wanting to be recognised for achievements, even lauded for the good one does. This appears to the case for the Pharisee in the Gospel, who, interestingly, initially defines and describes himself by what he is *not*: grasping, unjust and adulterous. His positive claims follow. He fasts twice a week and pays tax. Is he seeking status and reward for doing the minimum, what is expected?

The tax collector's starting point is unworthiness: 'God, be merciful to me, a sinner' (Luke 18:13). Recognition of this enables the tax collector to build from ground zero, so to speak. The Pharisee sets the bar quite high to start with by enunciating a series of presumptions about how he leads his life. The day-to-day life of a Christian must not be based on presumptions which acknowledge the minimum, but on a ground-zero recognition that even though I am a sinner I have the potential to improve and do good. It is not about status, but about recognising and acknowledging that sinner though I am God has called me, yes me, to do good. *Se Cristo videsse …*

---

*Social networking, while it certainly has some potentially valuable uses is, sadly, much more likely to be viewed as one of the most sinister developments in world history, making the controllers of the social networks the richest and most powerful people in the world … and making billions of people fritter their lives away with keeping their 'status' up to date. Never forget, if you're on Facebook too much, your status is always LOSER!*

Anonymous author writing under the name
Adam Weishaupt

---

**In the parish, family and workplace, how much are you concerned by status?**

# THE FOURTH WEEK
## OF LENT

# THE SUNDAY OF THE FOURTH WEEK IN LENT

*'And finally I am happy to offer as my personal tribute and gift to the Shrine of Knock a Rose in gold which will remain as my testimony of gratitude to Mary, "the Mother of the heavenly and the earthly Church". Praised be Jesus Christ!'*

Pope John Paul II, 30 September 1979

*Joshua 5:9–12 The People of God keep the Passover on their entry into the promised land*

*Psalm 34:2–7 Taste and see that the Lord is good*

*2 Corinthians 5:17–21 God reconciled us to himself through Christ*

*Luke 15:1-3, 11-32 Your brother here was dead and has come to life*

In French, the Fourth Sunday of Lent is known as *Mi-Carême*, mid-Lent Sunday. Other names for this day include Laetare Sunday (from the Latin words of the entrance antiphon at Mass, *Laetare Jerusalem*, 'Rejoice Jerusalem'), Refreshment Sunday (because you were allowed to relax your Lenten fast) or Rose Sunday. This last epithet is said to derive either from the rose-coloured vestments worn on this day, or from the practice of a golden rose being given by a pope to Catholic sovereigns, or, more recently, to significant churches or shrines. The rose was blessed on this day, hence the name *Dominica de Rosa*.

It is also known as Mothering Sunday. Early Christians in England held the Fourth Sunday of Lent in honour of the Virgin Mary, Mother of Christ. People commonly returned to their local church or cathedral, their 'mother' church, and were said to have gone 'a-mothering'. Young girls and boys in domestic service in manor houses and castles were allowed one day off a year to visit family. They brought gifts to be placed at the altar in their 'mother' church and then visited their own mothers, bringing them flowers and cakes and doing all the housework for them.

The idea of going home is at the heart of the well-known parable of the prodigal son. The younger son comes to his senses and returns to his father: 'He was lost and is found.' The welcome the son receives must be at the heart of the Christian ministry of welcome. Surely the Church should always be a place of welcome, and not only a place where everyone is welcome but where each one of us ensures the warmth and genuine nature of the welcome, and not just one day a year, but always.

> *Once a person learns to read the signs of love and thus to believe it, love leads him into the open field wherein he himself can love. If the prodigal son had not believed that the father's love was already waiting for him, he would not have been able to make the journey home – even if his father's love welcomes in a way he never would have dreamed of. The decisive thing is that the sinner has heard of a love that could be, and really is, there for him; he is not the one who has to bring himself into line with God; God has always already seen in him, the loveless sinner, a beloved child and has looked upon him and conferred dignity upon him in the light of this love.*
>
> Hans Urs von Balthasar, 1905–1988

**Have you ever felt unwelcomed or been unwelcoming?**

# THE MONDAY OF THE FOURTH WEEK IN LENT

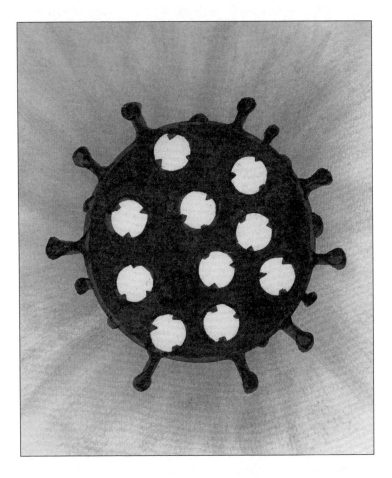

*2019-nCoV acute respiratory disease was the interim name initially given by the World Health Organization to what became the COVID-19 pandemic. The official name became coronavirus disease caused by the virus SARS-CoV-2 (severe acute respiratory syndrome coronavirus 2).*

*Isaiah 65:17–21 No more will the sound of weeping or the sound of cries be heard*

*Psalm 29:2, 4–6, 11–13 I will extol you, Lord, for you have raised me up*

*John 4:43–54 Go, your son is living*

If the year 2020 and then into 2021 taught us anything, it was that things can never be the same again. At the start of the coronavirus pandemic we might all have been thinking 'When will things get back to normal?' Then perhaps we began to wonder what 'the new normal' or even 'the difficult normal' might be. Snappy slogans traced an at-times-confusing trajectory: first, we had 'Stay at home, protect the NHS, save lives', and then, once it was safe to go outside, it was 'Stay alert, control the virus, save lives'. Then the Prime Minister introduced what he called a 'pretty punchy' new slogan, 'Hands, face, space', and in August 2020 the nation was encouraged to 'Eat out to help out'.

No slogan can hide the dramatic reality or soften the impact of something that changed everybody's lives. Everyone will have their own story to tell, be it the harrowing experience of a loved one dying in isolation, the anxiety of being furloughed, or simply not being able to hug someone.

Difficult though it may sound, and they may be but crumbs of comfort for some, one must not forget the positive stories. Many people felt a sense of community, a sense of neighbourliness they had not experienced before. Many churches discovered a new way of connecting, literally, using modern technology. Many people reset the compass of their lives to focus on values to which they had paid little attention before March 2020. Welcome to the new era of the challenging normal.

A new era, the era indicated by the prophet Isaiah, was ushered in by Jesus: 'For look, I am going to create new heavens and a new earth, the past will not be remembered and will no more come to mind ... The sound of weeping shall not be heard [in Jerusalem], nor the sound of a shriek' (65:17, 19). In John's Gospel, the court official asks Jesus to cure his son, and when he gets home he discovers that the boy began to recover precisely at the time Jesus said 'Go, your son is living' (4:50).

The new normal, the challenging normal, is that Jesus makes a difference. The invitation extended to all of us is to allow him to make a difference in our lives, so that we make a difference for others.

*The Lord asks us and, in the midst of our tempest, invites us to reawaken and put into practice that solidarity and hope capable of giving strength, support and meaning to these hours when everything seems to be floundering. The Lord awakens so as to reawaken and revive our Easter faith. We have an anchor: by his Cross we have been saved. We have a rudder: by his Cross we have been redeemed. We have a hope: by his Cross we have been healed and embraced so that nothing and no one can separate us from his redeeming love. In the midst of isolation when we are suffering from a lack of tenderness and chances to meet up, and we experience the loss of so many things, let us once again listen to the proclamation that saves us: he is risen and is living by our side. The Lord asks us from his Cross to rediscover the life that awaits us, to look towards those who look to us, to strengthen, recognise and foster the grace that lives within us. Let us not quench the wavering flame (cf. Isa. 42:3) that never falters, and let us allow hope to be rekindled ... Embracing the Lord in order to embrace hope: that is the strength of faith, which frees us from fear and gives us hope.*

Pope Francis, 27 March 2020

**How can Jesus make your life different every day?**

# The Tuesday of the Fourth Week in Lent

*The Code of Hammurabi is one of the oldest law codes, dating from c. 1745 BCE.*

*The stele depicts Hammurabi (standing) receiving the royal insignia from Shamash and is housed in the Louvre Museum, Paris. The Code contains 282 laws, including one of the earliest examples of the presumption of innocence and a minimum wage for workers.*

*Ezekiel 47:1-9, 12 I saw a stream of water coming from the Temple, bringing life to all wherever it flowed*

*Psalm 46:2-3, 5-6, 8-9 The Lord of hosts is with us: the God of Jacob is our stronghold*

*John 5:1-3, 5-16 The man was cured at once*

Rules and regulations are very important. The Church itself has a 'hierarchy of truths', which is not to say that some truths are more important than others – it is actually a way of ordering the mysteries of faith in relation to the Creed.

Some English and Welsh laws are intriguing. It is illegal to sell fried fish on Sundays, so no fish and chips next time you find yourself a little peckish at the seaside on a Sunday afternoon. Or, if you happen to be in York, be aware that it is illegal to kill a Scotsman carrying a bow and arrow within the city walls … but this law does not apply on a Sunday.

I remember a parish priest saying to me 'How easy it is to have a firm grasp of the non-essentials' – to give undue prominence to matters which, in themselves, are not of the greatest importance. Many years ago, at the rehearsal a few days before a big wedding, the mother of the bride asked me if the green tabernacle veil could be changed on the day of the wedding so that it would not clash with the flowers. A firm grasp of the non-essentials indeed!

In the Gospel, the Jews are concerned because a man had carried his sleeping mat on the Sabbath: he broke the rules. Jesus' concern for the man was that he should have the ability to lead a normal life, and so he cures him, with the admonition 'do not sin anymore' (John 5:14).

Living a life of faith is not an automatic box-ticking

exercise or a matter of sticking to the non-essentials. It is about striving to lead a life free from sin, focused on the essential: a loving relationship with God, witnessed in love of God and neighbour.

> *I want to see a new translation of the Bible into the hearts and conduct of living men and women. I want an improved translation – or transference it might be called – of the commandments and promises and teachings and influences of the Book to the minds and feelings and words and activities of the men and women who hold on to it and swear by it and declare it to be an inspired book and the only authorised rule of life. That seems to me to be the only translation, after all, that will in the long run prove to be of any value … It is of no use making correct translations of words, if we cannot get the words translated into life.*
>
> William Booth,
> founder of the Salvation Army, 1829–1912

**Is faith a compendium of rules or a way of life?**

# THE WEDNESDAY OF THE FOURTH WEEK IN LENT

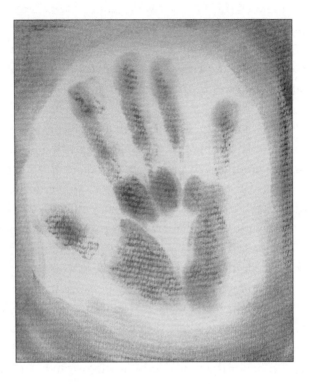

*Rome's Museum of the Holy Souls in Purgatory houses a collection of objects said to have been singed by the hands of those in purgatory. A book belonging to a Margherite Demmerlé bears the imprint of her mother-in-law's hand. She appeared to Margherite in 1815, thirty years after her death in 1785, asking her to undertake a pilgrimage to the Shrine of Our Lady of Mariental and have two Masses said for her there. After the pilgrimage, she appeared again to Margherite to tell her that she had been released from purgatory. When her daughter-in-law asked her for a sign, she put her hand on the book and left a burn mark.*

*Isaiah 49:8–15 I have appointed you as covenant of the people to restore the land*

*Psalm 145:8–9, 13–14, 17–18 The Lord is kind and full of compassion*

*John 5:17–30 As the Father raises the dead and gives them life, so the Son gives life to anyone he chooses*

In the early Church it was believed that forgiveness for mortal sins could only be obtained once after baptism and through a long and complicated process of penance. This could last a few weeks or even many years. For example, fornication incurred a seven-year penance, idolatry fifteen. Absolution and reconciliation took place at the end of Lent on completion of the penance. The fact that the Church maintained that this forgiveness could only be obtained once discouraged people from undergoing lengthy periods of penance in order to be forgiven. Catholic belief states that souls not totally free from sin wait in purgatory, where they have to be purified in order to achieve the holiness necessary to enter heaven. And so, in order to enhance their chances of getting straight to heaven and avoiding purgatory, many people waited until they were dying before being reconciled. This meant that there was an increase in deathbed confessions or even conversions – in finding faith at the finish line, as one modern-day author put it. Reconciliation became part of dying, not part of a Christian's life.

Perhaps one of the most famous deathbed conversions was that of the Roman Emperor Constantine. He was proclaimed Emperor by the army in York in the year 306. In 313, Christianity was accepted in the Roman Empire, and in 314 it became its official religion. Constantine himself remained a pagan, delaying his baptism because of his belief that sinning after baptism could only lead to the fires of hell. On his deathbed, in 337, he was baptised by Eusebius of Nicomedia.

The only certain things in this world are death and taxes. But faith must not be morbid preparation or apprehensive fear of death. There is the 'here and now' aspect, which is vitally important. The prophet Isaiah talks about 'the favourable time' and in John's Gospel Jesus emphasises the present: 'Amen, Amen I say to you, whoever listens to my words and believes in the one who sent me, has eternal life' (John 5:24). And again, he refers to the hour when the dead will hear the voice of the Son of God, but adds that it 'is here now' (v. 25).

The life of faith is the here and now. It is not about keeping pristine and safe from harm, like the contents of a museum. It is about witnessing to faith in a world so much in need of the gospel.

> We are not on earth as museum keepers, but to cultivate a flourishing garden of life and to prepare a glorious future.
>
> Saint Pope John XXIII, 1881–1963

**Is your faith focused on the beatific vision of eternal happiness or the 'here and now' of the gospel, or both?**

# THE THURSDAY OF THE FOURTH WEEK IN LENT

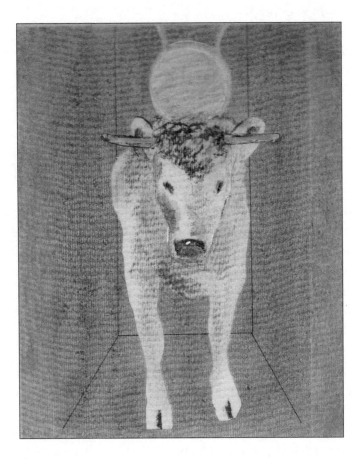

*Damien Hirst's* The Golden Calf *(2008). The formaldehyde-preserved British Charolais bull has horns and hooves cast in solid eighteen-carat gold. The work refers to the Israelites' worship of a golden calf, recounted in the Book of Exodus. The solid gold sun disc is a symbol of pagan deification. In 2008,* The Golden Calf *was bought in a Sotheby's auction for $13.4 million.*

*Exodus 32:7–14 Relent over this disaster for your people*

*Psalm 106:19–23 O Lord, remember me with the favour you show to your people*

*John 5:31–47 Your accuser will be Moses, in whom you have put your hope*

An old religious joke tells of a preacher caught in a flood and forced to flee to the roof of his house. He prayed to God to save him and a few minutes later a boat with two people in came by. 'Do you need help, sir?' came the cry from the boat. 'No, God will save me,' the preacher replied. The water continued to rise, as did the fervour of the preacher's prayers, and another boat came by. But again the preacher declined the invitation to get in the boat. 'God will save me,' he said. This happened a third time, with the same reaction from the preacher. The flood waters eventually swamped the house and the preacher was drowned. On his arrival in heaven, he said to God, 'Why didn't you save me?' God answered, 'What are you talking about? I sent you three boats!'

How tempting it is to see God in our own image and likeness and to reject any alternative: to accept only a personal salvation or rescue rather than one which offers three boats. This is moulding God into our shape, to do what we want so that God can be at our beck and call.

The Israelites make themselves a calf of molten metal and worship it. In John's Gospel, Jesus explains to the Jews that the testimony of John the Baptist, the works of Jesus himself, the very scriptures studied by the Jews, all point in one direction. But since these does not provide the answer they want, they refuse to believe in the one God has sent.

Some of life's solutions may not be the ones we want. This is when it is most tempting to seek a more comfortable answer elsewhere – to exchange, as the Psalmist says, 'their glory for the image of a bull that eats grass' (Ps. 106:20). The Lord's Prayer is probably the one prayed most often each and every day. And I do not think it says 'Your will be done as long, as it fits in with my nice little plan.'

*In the absence of Moses, the chosen people (the Israelites) quickly fell into idolatry and ended up worshipping a golden calf. This all happened a long time ago, we live in a very different world. There is no slavery today, no desert, no golden calf. But Scripture has an uncanny way of being timeless, of being relevant in every age and every place.*

*On the face of it there is no connection between Exodus and our time. No slavery today ... unless you count the people trapped in addiction, consumerism, and the endless struggle to make ends meet. No desert ... unless you count the people who feel lost and alone. No golden calf ... our time is certainly not short of false Gods, money, success, celebrity, possessions – and we haven't lost our fascination with the calf either! A few weeks ago at an auction in London somebody paid $13.5 million for an actual golden calf. What would the people wandering in the desert have made of that? That three and a half thousand years after their desert sculpture somebody would pay a king's ransom for a copy of it.*

Denis Brennan, Bishop of Ferns, Ireland

**Despite the witness of the scripture and of many individuals what is still difficult to believe about God and Jesus?**

# THE FRIDAY OF THE
# FOURTH WEEK IN LENT

A prison for heart and mind. *The Bolshevik Party of Vladimir Lenin seized power in the Soviet Union and established the first communist workers' state. 'Religion is the opium of the people,' wrote Karl Marx, and the Community Party began a campaign to discredit all gods, religious organisations and traditions. Anti-religious posters became a powerful medium used throughout the Soviet Union to proclaim the message that religion had no place in communist life.*

*Wisdom 2:1, 12–22 Let us condemn him to a shameful death*

*Psalm 34:16, 18, 19–21, 23 The Lord is close to the broken-hearted*

*John 7:1–2, 10, 25–30 They would have arrested him, but his hour had not yet come*

'The Macphersons were a family in no way remarkable. They were not rich or famous. Their women had been dowered with no special charms, and their men folk had never achieved greatness, nor, for that matter, had it been thrust upon them. The world in general was none the better for their existence – or an exalted idea of their own importance, which, perhaps, is a Scotch failing where "forbears" are irreproachable. The Macpherson "forbears" were, of course, that.'

These are the opening lines of an 1897 novel by Eliza Margaret Jan Humphreys entitled *Good Mrs Hypocrite: A Study in Self-righteousness.* The main character is a hypocritical spinster who hides behind her Christian piety to mask her own inadequacies.

'She [Mrs Hypocrite] was conscious of a keen regret that Tibbie Minch [the domestic] was not present, the [sermon] was so strangely applicable to her … It is always pleasant to see the failings of others held up to the light of day and riddled by bullets of home-truths.'

The Book of Wisdom presents us with the wonderful image of the disdainful godless lying in wait for the virtuous person. They criticise any claim that the virtuous has knowledge of God, what they perceive to be an aloof way of life, and condemn the virtuous to death. Fast forward two thousand years to the Soviet anti-religious propaganda waging war against all religion. *Plus ça change.*

Two things spring to mind. Firstly, criticisms such as those recounted in the Book of Wisdom abound and perhaps are even stronger today in a society where many would like to see faith and belief relegated to the private sphere. And in the face of that, it might be tempting to act as if faith and belief do make a person superior, to stand aloof from the actions of the godless 'and avoid [them] like filth' (Wis. 2:16). But what God rewards is holiness, not superiority.

*It is no longer possible to claim that religion should be restricted to the private sphere and that it exists only to prepare souls for heaven. We know that God wants his children to be happy in this world too, even though they are called to fulfilment in eternity, for he has created all things 'for our enjoyment' (1 Tim 6:17), the enjoyment of everyone. It follows that Christian conversion demands reviewing especially those areas and aspects of life 'related to the social order and the pursuit of the common good'.*

*Consequently, no one can demand that religion should be relegated to the inner sanctum of personal life, without influence on societal and national life, without concern for the soundness of civil institutions, without a right to offer an opinion on events affecting society. Who would claim to lock up in a church and silence the message of Saint Francis of Assisi or Blessed Teresa of Calcutta? They themselves would have found this unacceptable. An authentic faith – which is never comfortable or completely personal – always involves a deep desire to change the world, to transmit values, to leave this earth somehow better than we found it.*

Pope Francis, *Evangelii Gaudium*, n.182–183

**Is faith and belief something private and superior, or a call to service in the secular world?**

# THE SATURDAY OF THE FOURTH WEEK IN LENT

James Bond films always include a meeting between 007 and the head of Q Division, the section of the British Secret Service which provides Bond with all sorts of gadgets to assist him in his spying escapades. Although Bond might be regaled with the latest that technology can offer, Cold War espionage had a more direct approach. Shortly before the start of World War II, a German spy was caught in Russia with a textbook on political economy. Hidden inside was a Hungarian Liliput Kal 1925 6.35-calibre pistol.

*Jeremiah 11:18–20 I was like a trustful lamb being led to the slaughterhouse*

*Psalm 7:2–3, 9–12 O Lord, my God, I take refuge in you*

*John 7:40–52 Is the Messiah to come from Galilee?*

Do not judge a book by its cover, goes the adage. To do so, of course, is to make assumptions about the content, possibly even the author, with no evidential basis. However, I do not think I would be rushing out to buy *How Green Were the Nazis? Nature, Environment and Nation in the Third Reich* or *Anybody Can Be Cool ... But Awesome Takes Practice*. Maybe I am just reading the wrong type of books!

Of course, it is obvious that I have immediately fallen into the trap of making judgements based on my own prejudices or parameters of judgement: there will be people who would find the aforementioned books interesting. But because I am not one of them, I am poking fun, and do not accept their inherent merit and value.

Some of Jesus' critics appear to have judged him by his geography: 'Is the Messiah to come from Galilee?' (John 7:41). Others question his lack of suitable references: 'Have any of the authorities of the Pharisees believed in him?' (7:48).

Pope Francis has almost become synonymous with a statement he made during a press conference on his return flight from celebrating World Youth Day in Rio de Janeiro in 2013: 'If someone is gay and is searching for the Lord and has goodwill, then who am I to judge him?' As the Psalmist says, 'God is a judge, just, and powerful, patient and not finding fault every day' (Ps. 7:12); the prophet Jeremiah writes 'O

Lord Sabaoth whose judgement is righteous, you test the mind and the heart …' (11:20).

> *Our reaction to other persons, especially those with whom we do not agree, ought always to be characterised by a willingness to show people respect; to be careful not to damage another person's good name; to affirm what is good in another; never to be rude and insulting. The spirit of the Pharisee lurks in each one of us, tempting us to sit in judgement on others and even to seek to exclude them from the church.*
>
> Cardinal Basil Hume, 1923–1999

**Are you judgemental?**

# THE FIFTH WEEK
OF LENT

# Sunday of the Fifth Week in Lent

*The Tokyo 2020 Olympic medals were manufactured using precious metal extracted from small electronic devices donated by the public. More than 78,995 tons of used gadgets were collected by local authorities in Japan, including 6.21 million used mobiles. The front of the medal shows Nike, the Greek goddess of victory, in front of the Panathinaikos Stadium in Athens.*

*Isaiah 43:16–21 Look, I am about to do something new, for I am giving water in the desert for my people to drink*

*Psalm 125 What great deeds the Lord worked for us! Indeed, we were glad*

*Philippians 3:8–14 Reproducing the pattern of his death, I have accepted the loss of everything for Christ*

*John 8:1–11 Let the one among you who is without sin be the first to throw a stone at her*

At school, I used to do cross-country running; now, much more advanced in years, I occasionally go jogging. A number of funny, even painful incidents spring to mind: a match against another school, squelching through mud so deep that I lost one running shoe; one Boxing Day, going out for a run in hi-vis gear bought for me by my wife and badly twisting an ankle in the woods. There was no one around to see me in my bright new kit, so I hobbled painfully back to the car. Yes, I had forgotten my mobile phone, too!

The scriptures are no stranger to sporting metaphors, the most famous probably being St Paul's valedictory statement in the Second Letter to Timothy: 'I have fought the good fight, I have finished the race' (2 Tim. 4:7). There is also the admonition to the people of Corinth: 'Do you not know that, though all the runners in the stadium take part in the race, only one of them gets the prize? Run like that: to win' (1 Cor. 9:24).

The well-worn cliché about faith being a journey is absolutely correct. Becoming a Christian is not a point of arrival, but a start. Baptism should not be seen as a means to claim certain prerogatives or rights, but a statement about the duties and responsibilities of a Christian in today's world. St Paul makes this very clear in his message to the people of Philippi: 'Not that I have secured [the goal of resurrection] already, nor yet reached my goal; but I am still pursuing it, in the attempt to take hold of the prize for which Christ Jesus took hold of me. Brothers and sisters, I do not reckon myself as having taken hold of it; but one thing is that forgetting all that lies behind me, and straining forward to what lies ahead, I am racing towards the finishing-point to win the prize of God's heavenly call in Christ Jesus' (Phil. 3:12-14).

*Religious practices play a vital role in supporting our personal and spiritual development. By the sacrament of baptism, each one of us got an exclusive membership of the best spiritual gym in the world, offering the best spiritual equipment, namely the Catholic Church. The Eucharist is the best food supplement, the sacrament of Confirmation provides the best personal trainer, the Holy Spirit. The sacrament of Reconciliation is our best spiritual physio when we hurt ourselves and others, while the sacrament of the Sick strengthens us when we become weak. The sacrament of Matrimony teaches us teamwork, while the sacrament of Orders (priesthood) gives us support team members. But attending this spiritual gym is not an end in itself. It serves the second part of Jesus' manifesto: 'the kingdom of heaven has come near'.*

Father Tad Turksi, St Joseph's Church, Aberdeen

**Is your journey of faith a start or a finish, a marathon or a sprint?**

# THE MONDAY OF THE FIFTH WEEK IN LENT

On 11 October 1836, the Clarendon – a ship from the Caribbean – struck rocks at the foot of Blackgang Chine on the Isle of Wight in gale-force winds. Twenty-three lives were lost, as well as an exotic cargo of rum, coconuts and turtles. Two years later, work began on building a lighthouse, which came into operation in 1840. When the cows on the Downs first saw its light, it is said they stampeded in fear. St Catherine's lighthouse was one of the first in the world to be powered by electricity when arc lamps were installed in 1888. They could be seen for an incredible eighteen miles.

*Daniel 13:1–9, 15–17, 19–30, 33–62 Have I to die, innocent as I am?*

*Psalm 23 Though I should walk in the valley of the shadow of death no evil would I fear*

*John 8:12–20 I am the light of the world*

'A camel is a horse designed by committee.' These words are attributed to Sir Alec Issigonis, a British car designer who worked for Austin and Morris Motors Limited and went on to design the Mini, one of the most loved cars of all time. To honour his success, Alec was knighted in 1969. Just over thirty years later, General Motors launched what it believed to be a 'head-turner', a sexy, sit-up-and-be-noticed, must-have car – the 2001 Pontiac Aztek. Here was a car designed by committee with input from focus groups, designers, financiers, marketing experts and many more. After four years of dismal sales, production was discontinued, with the Aztek labelled as one of the ugliest cars, if not inventions, of all time.

The hymn 'The Lord Is My Shepherd', a rendition of Psalm 23, one of the best-known of all the psalms, could also be labelled the work of a committee. Francis Rous (1579–1659) published a book of Psalms in 1641. The text had to be submitted to the Long Parliament and a committee of translators, who deliberated for six years and made extensive alterations to the texts, so much so that perhaps only 10 per cent of Rous's original survives.

The Lord as a shepherd and Jesus as the light of the world are two memorable, familiar images. But they are not really images – they are reality. Psalm 23 is about the shepherd who always accompanies me and who provides security and guidance: 'Your crook and your staff will give me comfort' (v. 4). In John's Gospel, Jesus tells the people that he is the 'light of the world; anyone who follows me will not be walking in the dark, but will have the light of life' (8:12).

The message of the scriptures is of great comfort, particularly in times of distress and darkness. The Lord is not absent; he does not leave us lost and alone; he is the loving shepherd, the guiding light which pierces even the deepest darkness, the most impenetrable mist of despair.

*In the midst of Lent, here comes Psalm 23. The good shepherd walks with you in the midst of your troubles. The darkness may not be changed, but you are changed because in the shadow, we find we are not alone. How powerful is that? With talk of social isolation and social distancing becoming key phrases; when we, as Christians, used to communion and sharing, and being together, find ourselves fragmented individually, and splintered communally, by this virus, here is the good shepherd telling us, 'I am with you.' Even in the dark valley, with deathly things all around, 'Thou art with me.'*

*In the valley of the shadow of death, in the valley of extreme darkness, in the place of our deepest troubles and fears, the place where we think no one will ever accompany us, the shepherd is there. Not to lead us away from that place, but to walk us right through it. 'We face the darkness, but it holds no power over us because we are in the presence of the Lord.' 'Psalm 23 knows that there is evil in the world, but it is not feared. Confidence in God is the new orientation.'*

Sermon at Morningside Parish Church,
Edinburgh, 22 March 2020

**Are there times when you have felt the comfort of the Lord as shepherd and light in the darkness?**

# THE TUESDAY OF THE FIFTH WEEK IN LENT

*A new word was added to the* Oxford English Dictionary *in April 2020: Covid-19.*

*Lives were changed by the pandemic as people waited in hope for the 'new normal' to arrive. Language changed, too, as society got to grips with social distancing, self-isolation, quarantines, lockdowns, key workers, covidiots, staycations, second waves, coronacoasters and bubbles. Churches were closed and only gradually reopened in accordance with strict government and ecclesial guidance. Change led to the 'difficult normal'.*

*Numbers 21:4–9 Anyone who is bitten and looks at the fiery serpent shall live*

*Psalm 102:2–3, 16–21 O Lord, hear my prayer and let my cry come to you*

*John 8:21–30 When you have lifted up the Son of Man, then you will know that I am He*

It has been said that people tend to tell jokes about things they find most difficult. If this is true, then change must be very tough. There is an abundance of religious jokes about change. 'How many [Jesuits, Benedictines … you can insert the name of any religious order] does it take to change a light bulb?' 'Three: one to pour the gin, one to pour the tonic, and one to phone the electrician.' The same question can be met with a dramatic response: 'What do you mean, "change"?'

Change is very hard. It can take us out of our comfort zone, pull the rug of normality from under our feet and leave us adrift without any of the usual securities on which we rely.

The Israelites who fled Egypt in search of the Promised Land must have felt something like this. In the wilderness, they vent their anger and focus their frustration on the most basic of all necessities: 'we are sick of this wretched food' (Num. 21:5). The Israelites want to go back to Egypt, where they remember the fish they used to eat for free, '[along with] the cucumbers, melons, leeks, onions and garlic' (Num. 11:5).

Change is also challenge and the response of faith must be based on trust. The Israelites were called to believe in the God who would lead them to the Promised Land, to the land flowing with milk and honey; those listening to Jesus are called to trust his claims that he is not of this world (John

8:23) and that he is of the Father (John 8:28), and they are called to believe in him.

Faith is not about the comfort of a nice lifestyle. It is about trusting, believing and witnessing to Jesus seven days a week.

Fifty days after Easter, the Church returns to what is liturgically termed 'Ordinary Time'. God's action in calling the Israelites to the Promised Land and Jesus' salvific work in being lifted up on the Cross mean that faith can never return to the ordinary. Nothing can be the same again.

*All the life of our diverse churches finds renewal and unity when we are reconciled afresh to God and so are able to reconcile others. A Christ-heeding life changes the church and a Christ-heeding church changes the world.*

*Yet at the same time the church transforms society when it takes the risks of renewal in prayer, of reconciliation and of confident declaration of the good news of Jesus Christ. There is every possible reason for optimism about the future of Christian faith in our world and in this country. Optimism does not come from us, but because to us and to all people Jesus comes and says 'Take heart, it is I, do not be afraid.' We are called to step out of our own traditions and places, and go into the waves, reaching for the hand of Christ. Let us provoke each other to heed the call of Christ, to be clear in our declaration of Christ, committed in prayer to Christ, and we will see a world transformed.*

Archbishop Justin Welby, 21 March 2013

**Is faith comforting or challenging?**

# THE WEDNESDAY OF THE FIFTH WEEK IN LENT

*The Smallest House in Great Britain lies at the end of a terrace of houses on the Welsh town of Conwy's quayside. It is just 183 centimetres (72 inches) wide by 310 centimetres (122 inches) high and has a floor area of 3.05 by 1.8 metres (10 by 5.9 feet). The sixteenth-century dwelling was occupied until May 1900 and the last person to live there was a local fisherman called Robert Jones, who happened to be 6 feet and 3 inches (about 1 metre 90 centimetres) tall. The rooms were too small for him to stand up in fully and he was eventually forced to move out when the council declared the house unfit for human habitation.*

*Daniel 3:14–20, 24–25, 28 He has sent his angel to rescue his servants*

*Canticle: Daniel 3:52–56 To you glory and praise for evermore*

*John 8:31–42 So if the Son sets you free, you will indeed be free*

I am always wary when I read something about the 'average' person. Maybe I am just not 'average'. DIY research suggests that the 'average' British person will live in eleven different homes over his or her lifetime but settle just thirty-seven miles from where he or she grew up. First-time buyers have an average age of twenty-seven and average first house is a two-bed terrace property with an average price of £184,000 (unless, of course, you live in London, where the average is a two-bed flat costing an average of a lot more than £184,000). All those house moves means a lot of packing and unpacking, and I have heard of people who, in packing up their house ready for another move, find boxes still unpacked from when they moved in!

Much has been written about the difference between a house and a home. A house is really a roof and four walls – a building. A home is something more intangible. It represents comfort and safety. I am sure you have heard or even used the phrase 'This is where I most feel at home.' When people move into a new house, thoughts naturally turn to furnishing it, ensuring the kitchen is well equipped, and so on. Essential items for essential living, many would claim.

In John's Gospel, Jesus suggests that at the heart of every home should be his word: 'If you remain in my word, you are truly my disciples; you will come to know the truth, and the truth will set you free' (8:31–32). A house may be built on concrete, but a home is founded on the Word of God, which provides comfort and security and a message of truth.

> *The Bible is the written word of God, and because it is written it is confined and limited by the necessities of ink and paper and leather. The Voice of God, however, is alive and free as the sovereign God is free. 'The words that I speak unto you, they are spirit, and they are life.' The life is in the speaking words. God's word in the Bible can have power only because it corresponds to God's Word in the universe. It is the present Voice which makes the written word powerful. Otherwise it would lie locked in slumber within the covers of a book.*
>
> Aiden Wilson Tozer, American pastor, 1897–1963

**How is the Word of God heard in your home?**

# THE THURSDAY OF THE FIFTH WEEK IN LENT

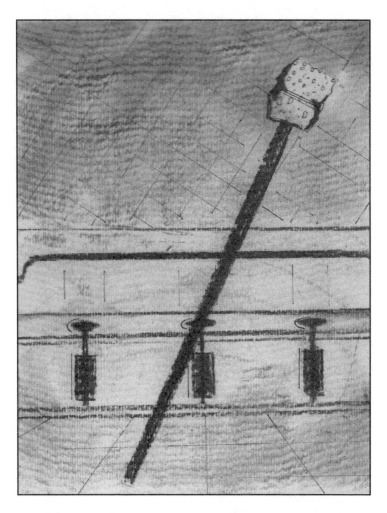

*Replica of an ancient Roman* xylospongium *or* tersorium, *a sponge on a stick. The word comes from the Greek* xylon *(stick) and* spongos *(sea sponge).*

*Genesis 17:3–9 You will become the father of many nations*

*Psalm 105:4–9 The Lord remembers his covenant for ever*

*John 8:51–59 Your father Abraham rejoiced that he should see my day*

The idiomatic verb 'to get the wrong end of the stick' is one that most of us will have heard and probably used. Maybe in the middle of a profound conversation or perhaps an office meeting, after listening to someone waxing eloquently about a particular issue, someone might have the courage to pipe up and say 'But you've got completely the wrong end of the stick.'

The origins of this popular maxim are a long way from polite office chit-chat, as was revealed to me many years ago during a guided tour of Rome's ancient port of Ostia Antica, founded in the seventh century BCE. Maybe it satisfies a particular lavatorial sense of humour, but tours always include the communal toilets, where a water system delivered water continuously into troughs between a line of marble seats, discharging the waste into the River Tiber. Romans in their togas simply sat on the seats (slaves were sometimes employed to warm the marble by sitting there first) while they did what they had to do, possibly chatting to the person sitting on the piece of marble next to them. The hole in the seat made necessary cleansing – using a sponge-on-a-stick – easy, but, as the guide said to our group, woe betide you if you got the wrong end of it!

In John's Gospel, the Jews regularly seem, at worst, to get the wrong end of the stick, or, at best, just to misunderstand what Jesus is talking about. He says those who keep his word will never see death; they say Abraham and the prophets are dead, and they adhered to God's word. He says that Abraham has seen 'my day'; they say Jesus is not even fifty years old and is claiming to have seen Abraham.

It is easy for all of us not only to get the wrong end of the stick but once we have done so to rush headlong into ensuring that 2 + 2 = 5 and to become judgemental. The Jews in the Gospel picked up stones to throw at Jesus. How easy it is for us to launch verbal missiles in the direction of those we have been quick to judge. The first word of the Rule of St Benedict is 'Obsculta' – 'Listen'. Although the Rule was written perhaps 1,500 years ago, how well we would do to pay heed today even to just its opening word.

*Jesus does not want selfish Christians who follow their own ego, who do not talk to God. Nor does he want weak Christians, Christians who have no will of their own, 'remote-controlled' Christians incapable of creativity, who always seek to connect with the will of someone else and are not free. Jesus wants us free. And where is this freedom created? It is created in dialogue with God in the person's own conscience. If a Christian is unable to speak with God, if he cannot hear God in his own conscience, he is not free, he is not free ... The conscience is the interior place for listening to the truth, to goodness, for listening to God; it is the inner place of my relationship with him, the One who speaks to my heart and helps me to discern, to understand the way I must take and, once the decision is made, to go forward, to stay faithful.*

Pope Francis, 30 June 2013

**How easy is it to listen and how do you exercise the art of listening?**

# THE FRIDAY OF THE FIFTH WEEK IN LENT

The swingometer first appeared on British television during the 1955 general election when it was used to show the swing in the two constituencies of Southampton, Itchen and Southampton Test. The original device was a cardboard arrow and arc propped on a desk. The swingometer was first used in national broadcasts in 1959 and at the 1970 general election for the first time showed the traditional party colours of red for Labour and blue for Conservative. Today, the swingometer involves elaborate virtual graphics displayed on the wall of the TV studio.

*Jeremiah 20:10–13 The Lord is at my side like a mighty hero*

*Psalm 18:2–7 In my anguish I called to the Lord and he heard my voice*

*John 10:31–42 They again sought to arrest him, but he escaped from their hands*

Being a Christian in the UK is not very trendy. In a YouGov poll at the end of 2020, although 56 per cent of people interviewed still regarded the UK as a Christian country, only 34 per cent professed to be Christian themselves, and 55 per cent claimed to belong to no religion at all. Only 27 per cent claimed to believe in a god and only 28 per cent believed Jesus Christ to be the Son of God. And the chances of people being swayed by religious leaders seemed remote: 71 per cent said they paid no attention to the Christmas and Easter messages of the Pope, while the Archbishop of Canterbury did not fare much better: 66 per cent said they paid no attention to his messages.

Of course, statistics can make for a topic for conversation within the comfort of our own living rooms, churches or even workplaces. But some statistics can make grim reading. Every day, eight Christians are killed because of their decision to follow Jesus. Tonight, by the time you lie down to go to sleep, eight people will have died for their faith. Of course, these are the deaths we know about – in reality, the daily figure is likely to be higher.

The prophet Jeremiah (born c. 640 BCE) is attacked and criticised by those trying to catch him out because of his faith as they watch out for his downfall: 'Perhaps he will be tricked into error. Then we shall get the better of him and then we can take our revenge!' (Jer. 20:10). Jeremiah firmly believes that the Lord is with him, 'like a mighty hero'. This is not some comic-book Captain Marvel but the Lord who 'delivers the life of the needy from the hands of evildoers' (20:13).

There is a trend, perhaps a desire, to relegate religion to the private sphere. There are times when it can be uncomfortable to profess to being a Christian – and this in a society where the chances of you actually being killed for your faith are really very slim. But for comfort's sake, it might be tempting to keep your head below the parapet.

That is not a life of faith. Jeremiah trusted in the Lord. He did not place his hope in the fact that the noisy critics might go away. Faith for Jeremiah, and for all of us, is not about statistics but about belief in and witness of 'you Lord, my strength, my rock, my fortress, my saviour' (Ps. 17:1–2).

*It is Jesus in fact that you seek when you dream of happiness; he is waiting for you when nothing else you find satisfies you; he is the beauty to which you are so attracted; it is he who provokes you with that thirst for fullness that will not let you settle for compromise; it is he who urges you to shed the masks of a false life; it is he who reads in your hearts your most genuine choices, the choices that others try to stifle. It is Jesus who stirs in you the desire to do something great with your lives, the will to follow an ideal, the refusal to allow yourselves to be grounded down by mediocrity, the courage to commit yourselves humbly and patiently to improving yourselves and society, making the world more human and more fraternal.*

Saint Pope John Paul II, 19 August 2000

**Are there times when you are afraid or unwilling to profess to being a Christian?**

# THE SATURDAY OF THE FIFTH WEEK IN LENT

*The biggest jigsaw puzzle in the world is called Memorable Disney Moments and depicts ten scenes from the most popular Disney films, from* Snow White and the Seven Dwarves *in 1937 to* The Lion King *in 1994. The 40,320-piece puzzle measures 22 feet (6.7 metres) in length and over 6 feet (182 centimetres) in width, covers nearly 140 square feet (13 square metres), weighs approximately 44 pounds (20 kilograms), and takes an estimated 600 hours to complete. And it costs a mere $599.99, excluding tax and shipping costs.*

*Ezekiel 37:21–28 I will make them into one nation*

*Canticle: Jeremiah 31:10–13 The Lord will guard us as a shepherd guards his flock*

*John 11:45–56 To gather together into one the dispersed children of God*

I remember a parish priest who had a very sweet tooth and loved tucking into chocolates, particularly Christmas selection boxes and Easter eggs. As he did so, he would remark with great satisfaction 'All this, and heaven too.' Now, I do not think he was referring to the 1940 American film of the same name, based on a true story of the Duc de Choiséul-Praslin, a French politician who was accused of the brutal murder of his wife in 1847. (Praslin committed suicide while under house arrest and to this day the case remains one of France's most famous unsolved murder cases.)

No, I do not think he was referring to that. I think it was a sort of 'Imagine all this enjoyment! Satisfaction on earth, and we have been promised the joys of heaven, too.'

It is important to keep this 'big picture' in mind, especially in times of doubt and despair, when we wonder what on earth life is all about and where we are going. The prophet Ezekiel provides a message of comfort to the Israelites who underwent the siege of Jerusalem and subsequent deportation to Babylon (586 BCE), promising a glorious future back on their own soil: 'I shall make a covenant of peace with them, an eternal covenant with them. I shall resettle them and make them grow; I shall set my sanctuary among them for ever. I shall make my home above them; I shall be their God and they will be my people' (Ezek. 37:26–28).

This is the bigger picture – the future joy to hold on to in the midst of despair. In John's Gospel the high priest, Caiaphas, unwittingly points to that bigger picture which reminds us all what this Jesus-event is about: 'You know nothing at all; you have not worked out that it is better for you that one man should die for the people, rather than the whole nation should perish' (11:49–50).

That is precisely what Jesus has done for all of us. He has taken on our sins, our faults and failings and let himself be crucified in order to save us. All this, and heaven too.

> *If you insist on having your own way, you will get it. Hell is the enjoyment of your own way forever. If you really want God's way with you, you will get it in heaven, and the pains of purgatory will not deter you, they will be welcomed as means to that end.*
>
> Dante Alighieri, 1265–1321

**In times of doubt and despair where and how do you feel comforted in faith?**

# HOLY WEEK

# PALM SUNDAY OF THE LORD'S PASSION

*At the centre of St Peter's Square in Rome stands an 85-foot (26-metre) high 350-ton obelisk, erected on 10 September 1586. The obelisk was brought from its site nearby in the Circus of Nero by 900 workers and 140 horses. Thousands of people gathered to watch it being placed upright and Pope Sixtus V announced that there had to be total silence while the work was carried out: anyone who spoke would be put to death. As the obelisk was being raised, the ropes began to fray and the obelisk started to sway. Benedetto Bresca, a sailor from the Italian Riviera town of Sanremo-Bordighera who was watching the event, shouted out 'L'aiga ae corde!' – 'Water on the ropes!' The chief engineer heeded the advice, the ropes became taut again and the work was completed successfully. As a reward, Pope Sixtus gave Benedetto and his descendants the privilege of supplying palms to the Vatican for Palm Sunday and to this day the palm fronds used in the Vatican on Palm Sunday come from Bordighera.*

*The Procession*
*Luke 19:28–20 Blessed is he who is coming as King in the name of the Lord!*

*The Mass*
*Isaiah 50:4–7 I did not turn away my face from insult and spitting – I know that I shall not be shamed*

*Psalm 22:8-9, 17–20, 23–24 My God, my God, why have you forsaken me?*

*Philippians 2:6-11 He humbled himself, but God raised him high*

*The passion of our Lord Jesus Christ Luke 22:14 – 23:56*

Just like that of getting the Christmas tree and decorations down from the attic, there was also a bit of a ritual in our house on Palm Sunday. Dad would stick up in the front-room window an A4 poster with an outline of Jesus on the Cross with the words 'This is Holy Week.' So, after five weeks of fasting, we have reached the real meaning of Lent. If this final week is a reminder of what faith is, then 'Holy Week' seems a bit of an inadequate description. For the Eastern Catholic Churches, this is 'The Week of Salvation'. It is not about celebrating old rituals: it is a week in which we celebrate the new life Jesus won for us by his passion, death and resurrection.

Of course, being an irreverent little altar boy, I did not really understand all of that. Palm Sunday was a great opportunity to collect up all the palm branches left in church and have mock sword fights with them on the way home! And then the palm branches would be put behind a holy picture hanging over the fireplace, as if they were peeking out, watching over us, until they would be replaced on the next Palm Sunday.

What might have seemed a quaint tradition of sticking palms behind a picture for a year now seems quite profound. Jesus was welcomed into Jerusalem on a donkey by people lining the streets and praising God: 'Blessed is he who is coming as King in the name of the Lord! Peace in heaven and glory in the highest heavens!' (Luke 19:38). Bringing our palms home from church makes us part of that crowd; we welcome Jesus into our homes, with the palm branch a sign of our joy at his presence. In Luke's Gospel, the Pharisees ask Jesus to control his disciples. Perhaps they are making too much noise, too much commotion, in this noisy procession. Jesus tells the Pharisees that if the disciples do not cry out then the very stones will. This is the week that makes a difference, and the challenge today is to proclaim so with our lives, even be noisy by our witness.

*Yes, Jesus is exalted by the crowds. Yes, he is lifted up onto the back of a donkey so that he may be seen by all. Yes, in this moment he does appear to prosper. But we know what is to come.*

*Jesus will be lifted up, but on a cross of shame and suffering. Yes, he will prosper, but in an entirely different way: in being raised from the dead, prospering in a victory over death. Yes, he will rise to great heights, to be seated at the right hand of the Father in heaven. Yes, he will be exalted: by the voice of the faithful raised in praise and thanksgiving, even as we do this morning.*

*So, here are the questions that face each one of us: What is the praise that we seek? Whose acclaim is crucially important to us? What are the heights to which we aspire?*

*These days of Holy Week, starting today, are the moments in which we can recalibrate our ambitions.*

Cardinal Vincent Nichols,
Archbishop of Westminster, Palm Sunday 2019

**What is 'holy' about this week for you?**

# THE MONDAY OF HOLY WEEK

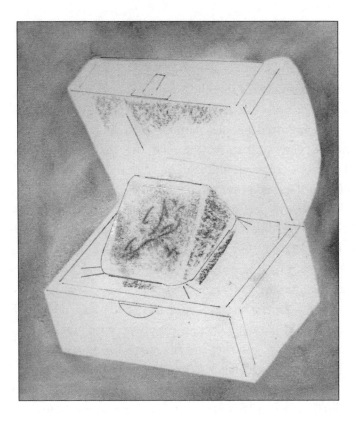

The world's most expensive soap was first made in 2013 in Tripoli, Lebanon, by the family-run Bader Hassen & Sons and was given as a gift to the first lady of Qatar. It costs a mere $2,800 a bar, contains 17 grams of 24-karat gold, a few grams of diamond powder, pure olive oil, organic honey, aged oud and dates. The CEO of the company described the soap as a delight for the senses: 'That kind of soap changes your shower from daily routine to pleasure ...[the soap] has a psychological and spiritual effect on the human being.'

*Isaiah 42:1–7 He will not cry out or raise his voice*

*Psalm 27:1–3, 13–14 The Lord is my light and my salvation*

*John 12:1–11 Leave her alone, so that she may keep this scent for the day of my burial*

It is sometimes said that the toughest job in comedy is that of the warm-up – the person who has to stand in front of one or two hundred people, perhaps even more, and entertain them as they wait to see the main act, the main attraction. Warm-ups are never quite famous, but the stars could not do without them and their preparation.

The early part of Holy Week has an air of preparation about it. We all know the main story, which will be narrated on Good Friday, but leading up to it are a few scene-setters which help maintain the atmosphere generated on Palm or Passion Sunday.

Judas Iscariot has had centuries of bad press. St Jude is the patron saint of hopeless cases simply because nobody would pray to him in case they got his name wrong and ended up praying to Judas instead. So he even gets the blame there.

Today's media would possibly accuse Judas of gesture politics, since in the story of Jesus' anointing at Bethany, he thinks the money used to buy the ointment could have been used to help the poor. But the Gospel passage carefully notes 'He said this, not because he cared about the poor, but because he was a thief; he was in charge of the common fund and used to steal from the contents' (John 12:6).

Leaving aside gesture politics, Jesus' response to critics of Mary, who had anointed his feet, is pointed: 'You have the poor with you always, you will not always have me' (12:8).

How easy it is to play gesture politics, to do good deeds when they will be noticed and provide a good photo opportunity.

But we *do* always have Jesus with us. We have Jesus in the poor, the marginalised, the vulnerable, the excluded. These may not look like the sort of people who usually sit at our dinner table, but they are always with us. They deserve our attention today if we are true Christians, not people for whom faith is a self-serving gesture.

> *Let's think of that moment when a woman washed the feet of Jesus with the nard, so expensive: it is a religious moment, a moment of gratitude, a moment of love. And he [Judas] stands apart with bitter criticism: 'But this could have been used for the poor!' This is the first reference that I have found, in the Gospel, to poverty as an ideology. The ideologue does not know what love is, because he does not know how to give himself.*
>
> Pope Francis, 27 March 2018

**How can faith and religious practice be an empty gesture?**

# THE TUESDAY OF HOLY WEEK

The flourishing industry of Etiquette Consultants sheds light on 'Etiquette for the Modern World' with lessons on how to enter the dining room, when to start eating, how to hold your cutlery properly, how to hold polite conversation, and when and how to excuse yourself from the table. If it is just Afternoon Tea you are interested in then your Etiquette Consultant will guide you through the rituals of a traditional British Tea Experience including a History of Afternoon Tea.

*Isaiah 49:1–6 I shall make you a light to the nations so that my salvation may reach to the ends of the earth*

*Psalm 71:1–6, 15, 17 My mouth will tell of your righteousness*

*John 13:21–33, 36–38 One of you will betray me; before the cock crows, you will have disowned me three times*

Some years ago, a computer software company invited me to a marketing event and lunch at one of London's very posh hotels. With some trepidation, I arrived at 11 a.m. as requested and was informed at the reception desk that I was to be taken to the champagne bar where the event was to begin. Now, I do like a glass of champagne, but at 11 a.m. on an empty stomach? Anyway, the event went very well, and at 1 p.m. the twelve invited guests were escorted by our hosts to the private dining room. *At last*, I thought. *Some food.* As we were shown to our places, I caught my breath and the colour drained from my face: in front of me was an array of cutlery, some pieces of which I had never seen before in my life. This was not going to be a positive experience. I spent a good part of the meal pretending to engage in social chit-chat when really I was trying to work out which piece of cutlery went with which piece of fine dining. Thankfully, more attention was being given to snappy computer graphics being shown on the screen than to my social ineptitude.

'Amen, Amen I say to you, one of you will betray me' (John 13:21). This must have been a chilling, dramatic moment for those gathered around the table with Jesus. He had just washed the disciples' feet, returned to his place and explained what he meant by service. And in their midst was the betrayer. "'It is the one for whom I dip the piece of bread and give to him.' Then dipping the piece of bread he gave it to Judas, son of Simon Iscariot' (13:26).

At the posh hotel, I was struggling. This was one of those meals where at each course the chef comes along to explain what has just been put in front of you. It is always a bad sign, I think, if someone has to explain what has been cooked because it may not be obvious. However, at the end of the day, the meal was good fun and the champagne was very nice.

Meals are not just about essential nourishment for the body. They are also social occasions, community occasions, family occasions. The earliest depiction of the Eucharist, in the catacombs of Priscilla in Rome, is a second-century fresco showing people reclined or seated at a table where there is a cup of red wine, a plate with five loaves and another with two fish. This fresco shows that from the outset Christians shared a table together, a fellowship meal. We do the same today, hopefully in our family home, and also gathered around the Table of the Lord, where we break bread, share communion, offer each other a sign of peace. Such occasions should be joyful celebrations of Jesus' presence, not a tension-filled event of betrayal, falling out and not speaking to one another.

*Sometimes we are like John: we have great moments of intimacy with Jesus, of deep prayer and unshakeable love for the Lord. Sometimes we are like Peter: we can be so pious and enthusiastic one moment, saying 'Master, I will lay down my life for you,' and then the next moment running away in fear. And then sometimes we can be like the silent Judas, rejecting the light and slinking off into the darkness. If we are honest, I think we've all had wonderful John moments, naïve Peter moments, and dark Judas moments. The sacrament of Confession helps us to turn away from those times we have been like Judas. And our Lenten practices of prayer, fasting and almsgiving help us to build up some courage and fortitude so that we don't run away, like Peter, at the sight of the Cross. I expect when John the beloved inclined his ear to Jesus' heart, Jesus knew John's weaknesses and fears. But drawing near to the Lord's heart changes us.*

Father Kevin Estabrook,
St Ignatius of Antioch Church, Cleveland, OH

**How do you make family meals and the Eucharist celebratory events today?**

# THE WEDNESDAY OF HOLY WEEK

Judas was filled with remorse at the condemnation of Jesus and threw the thiry pieces of silver into the Temple. 'Then he went away and hanged himself' (Matt. 27:5). *According to tradition, Judas hanged himself on a redbud tree, Cercis siliquastrum. As he did so, the tree's white flowers turned red in shame that Christ's betrayer had died on it. The Judas Tree, the Mediterranean Redbud, is native to the eastern Mediterranean and can be found in many areas of the Middle East, and in the northern and central regions of Israel.*

*Isaiah 50:4–9 I did not turn away my face from insult and spitting*

*Psalm 69:8–10, 21–22, 31, 33–34 In your great mercy, answer me, O God, with your salvation that never fails*

*Matthew 26:14–25 The Son of man is going to his fate, as it is written about him, but alas for that man by whom the Son of man is betrayed*

Judas Iscariot is centre stage on the day traditionally known as 'Spy Wednesday'. This is not a reference to a James Bond-esque modern-day tale of espionage but a simple act of betrayal and greed: for a price, Judas provided the wanted man, and once he had received his money he waited for the appropriate moment to betray him. In his *Divine Comedy*, Dante Alighieri (*c.* 1265–1321) places Judas in the lowest circle of hell, the circle made for traitors, where he is devoured eternally by a three-faced bat-winged devil. A bargain for thirty pieces of silver!

There are a variety of traditions associated with this day. In some villages in Poland, an effigy of Judas is thrown from a church steeple, dragged through the streets and stoned, and then drowned in a pond. In the Czech Republic, it was traditional to have chimneys swept in preparation for Easter and the day became known as Ugly Wednesday, Soot-Sweeping Wednesday or Black Wednesday. In Scandinavia, church bells were muffled, and wooden clappers – *dymbil* – were used instead until Easter. This was *Dymmelonsdagen*.

Every man has his price, and Spy Wednesday is clearly a manifestation of that. Although it is a cheap (no pun intended!) generalisation, I am often struck by professional footballers who might score a great goal for their team and, in celebration, kiss the club badge on the shirt in front of cheering and adoring fans. Some time later, that same footballer might sign a multi-million-pound contract with a new club. I know there are many complexities around multi-million-pound transfers, but the values of faith, loyalty and commitment can be truly tested, and not just in the world of professional football, but in the day-to-day life of religious practice, too. Judas was called by Jesus to follow him, but perhaps the price was too much. We, too, are called to follow Jesus, at all costs.

*Judas became the spokesman of all those who through the centuries would protest the ornamentation of the Christian cult and would feel that, when the best of gold and jewels were given to the God who made them, there was some slight made to the poor – not because they were interested in the poor, but because they were envious of that wealth.*
Archbishop Fulton J. Sheen, 1895–1979

**Have you been tempted to betray your faith?**

# Holy Thursday

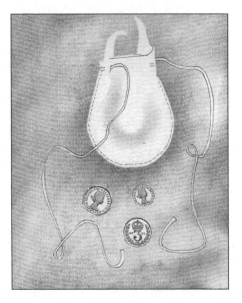

*Inspired by the gospel accounts of Jesus washing the disciples' feet, in the thirteenth century the royal family used to wash the feet of the poor and give money and gifts. Henry IV introduced the practice of giving the same number of gifts as his age. The tradition of the king or queen washing the feet of the poor disappeared in the eighteenth century, but food and clothing were still distributed. By the nineteenth century the monarch simply gave Maundy money. Maundy money is traditionally made of sterling silver and it bears the portrait of the Queen which appeared on the first coins of her reign in 1953. The recipients are elderly men and women chosen because of their Christian service to the Church and the community. There are as many recipients as there are years in the sovereign's age. Two purses are given: a red purse contains ordinary coins, a white purse contains Maundy coins, amounting to the same number of pence as the years of the sovereign's age.*

*Evening Mass of the Lord's Supper*

*Exodus 12:1–8, 11–14 Instructions concerning the Passover meal*

*Psalm 116:12–13, 15–18 The cup of blessing which we bless is fellowship in the blood of Christ*

*1 Corinthians 11:23–26 As often as you eat this bread and drink this cup, you are proclaiming the Lord's death*

*John 13:1–15 Now he showed how perfect his love was*

Well, Lent is over for another year. For far too long I used to think it ended on Easter Sunday morning and when I realised that it was actually at the start of the Mass of the Lord's Supper on Holy Thursday evening I wondered whether I should try to claim all those sweets I had given up unnecessarily for three extra days for all those years! Yes, Lent is over, but what this *really* means is that the focus shifts to the last days of Jesus' life on earth.

In many respects, today is like a big picture in which there is just too much going on. It is officially called Thursday of the Lord's Supper, since the evening celebration recalls the institution of the Eucharist, with the oldest account provided by St Paul and written in c. 57 CE: 'On the night he was betrayed, the Lord Jesus took some bread, and after he had given thanks, he broke it, and he said, "This is my body, which is for you; do this in remembrance of me." And in the same way with the cup after supper, saying, "This cup is the new covenant in my blood. Whenever you drink it, do this in remembrance of me"' (1 Cor. 11:24–25).

Then, of course, there is the washing of the feet, a ritual introduced in the fifth century, a reminder of Jesus' example of service. Over fifty years ago in my local parish the parish priest used to wash the feet of twelve altar servers. Senior servers would tell those present for the first time they might be 'lucky' enough to be chosen as Judas and, with straight faces, they said this meant that at the end of the foot-washing ceremony Judas would be thrown into the bath in the middle of the altar!

Today is also Maundy (from the Latin *mandatum*, meaning commandment) Thursday, from the words of Jesus recounted in John's Gospel after the washing of the feet: 'I give you a new commandment: that you love one another; you must also love one another just as I have loved you' (13:34).

For all the different elements in the liturgy there appears to be a clear theme uniting them all: humble service and self-giving. That is the example given to us by Jesus, and the example we are called to live out in our daily lives.

*I have great pleasure in sending you the Maundy Gift which, unfortunately, I am unable to distribute to you personally ... This ancient Christian ceremony, which reflects Jesus's instruction to his Disciples to love one another, is a call to the service of others, something that has been at the centre of my life. I believe it is a call to service for all of us. It is one of my most rewarding duties as Sovereign to observe this highly significant ceremony at such an important point in the Christian calendar. I know that you, as a Recipient of this year's Maundy Gift, will be as deeply disappointed as I am that it is not going ahead, while understanding the necessary decision in the current circumstances. However, this should not mean your invaluable contribution within the community goes unnoticed, and I am sending this Maundy Gift to thank you for your Christian service. My thoughts and prayers are with you and your families at this difficult time.*

Queen Elizabeth II, April 2020

**Which element of the Holy Thursday ceremony appeals to you most?**

# Good Friday

The Crucifixion *is an unusual combination of mosaic and painted fresco completed in 1955 in Oldham's Church of the Holy Rosary, Lancashire, by Georg Mayer-Marton. The large mosaic depicts the figure of Christ in golds* and tans against a dark blue cross and gold mandorla. *It was commissioned in 1955 following the Festival of Britain when public art came to be seen as a symbol of civic renewal and social progress. Mayer-Marton was born in Hungary in 1897 to an agnostic family of Jewish heritage. He studied art in Vienna and Munich and was prominent among Viennese artists, but fled Austria in 1938 after its annexation by Nazi Germany. He and his wife settled in England, and he taught for the Arts Council of Great Britain and then at the Liverpool College of Art. He died in 1960.*

*Isaiah 52:13 – 53:12 He was wounded for our rebellions*

*Psalm 31:2, 6, 12–13, 15–17, 25 Father, into your hands I commit my spirit*

*Hebrews 4:14–16, 5:7–9 He learnt obedience through his suffering and became for all who obey him the source of eternal salvation*

*John 18:1 – 19:42 The passion of our Lord Jesus Christ*

In Italian and French it is obvious: *Venerdì Santo* and *Le Vendredi Saint*. This day is *santo*, 'holy'. In English, the day is 'good', which seems a bit odd. We are all used to phrases such as 'That was a really good meal' or 'The weather's good', but the use of the adjective in these situations is not the same as its application to this day.

So what is 'good' about it? One suggestion is that the phrase is actually a corruption of 'God's Friday', from the German *Gottes Freitag*. More likely it comes from a time when the adjective 'good' referred to a day when a religious observance was held, a day revered as holy by the Church. In German-speaking countries, this day is known as *Karfreitag*. *Kar* comes from an Old High German word meaning 'grievance' or 'mourning', and so today could be roughly translated as 'Mourning Friday'. Good Friday, then, is a holy day, a day of mourning.

Increasingly, it has become a day like any other. Shops are open, sports fixtures go ahead (although horse racing on Good Friday was not allowed prior to 2013), and hot cross buns are devoured up and down the country.

But today is different. For example, it is the only day of the year on which the Eucharist is not celebrated. The churches are bare, silence fills the air, and at 3 p.m., the hour when liturgies traditionally begin in parishes, the ministers enter in silence and prostrate themselves or kneel for a time of silent prayer. Good Friday is different.

As a young altar server fifty years ago, for me, the day was certainly different because it meant being in church a lot and the services – the Liturgy of the Passion in the afternoon and the Stations of the Cross in the evening – seemed to go on for hours and hours. In fact, I remember one year fainting during the Stations of the Cross, the large candle I was carrying clattering to the floor, swiftly followed by my body. Not the most edifying of sights.

One phrase which sticks in my mind from the traditional meditations written by St Alphonsus Liguori (1696–1787) is from the last Station, the Burial of Jesus: 'Consider how the disciples, accompanied by his holy Mother, carried the body of Jesus to bury it. They closed the tomb, and all came sorrowfully away.' It seems such a sad ending. But in faith, we know this is only the beginning.

*He makes his way, station after station, through the believers and the atheists, the hopeful and the despairing, the rich and the poor, the happy families and the forlorn individuals. He is the object of scrutiny by curious onlookers, excited children, contemplative crowds. He passes through a gathering of nations, languages, and cultures, sowing on his way the question that every Christian must answer: 'And who do you say that I am?' He is nailed to the Cross, then placed in the tomb. The crowd disperses into the night, each person looking for the last station – the station that manifests itself in life's many twists and turns.*

*Tonight, Jesus passes among us on the Way of the Cross – just as he does every day on the streets of the world.*

Way of the Cross, World Youth Day,
Toronto, Canada, 26 July 2002

**How does Good Friday make a difference to you?**

# HOLY SATURDAY

*The Paschal Candle stand in Rome's Basilica of St Paul's Outside the Walls is just over 18 feet (5.6 metres) high and dates from the twelfth century. The decorations are divided into eight sections, including scenes from Christ's passion: Christ before Caiaphas, the mocking of Christ, Christ before Pilate, Pilate washing his hands, the crucifixion, the resurrection and the ascension.*

*Genesis 1:1- 2:2 God saw all he had made, and indeed it was very good*

*Psalm 104:1–2, 5–6, 10, 12–14, 24, 35 You send forth your spirit, O Lord, and renew the face of the earth*

*Genesis 22:1–18 The sacrifice of Abraham, our father in faith*

*Psalm 16:5, 8–11 Preserve me, God, for I take refuge in you*

*Exodus 14:15 – 15:1 The sons of Israel went on dry ground right into the sea*

*Exodus 15:1–6, 17–18 I shall sing to the Lord, he has triumphed in glory!*

*Isaiah 54:5–14 With everlasting love the Lord your redeemer has taken pity on you*

*Psalm 29:2, 4–6, 11–13 I will extol you, Lord, for you have raised me up*

*Isaiah 55:1–11 Come to me; listen, and you will live, and I shall make an everlasting covenant with you*

*Isaiah 12:2–6 Joyfully you will draw water from the springs of salvation*

*Baruch 3:9–15, 32 – 4:4 In the radiance of the Lord make your way to light*

*Psalm 19:8–11 You have the words of eternal life, O Lord*

*Ezekiel 36:16–18 I shall pour clean water over you and I shall give you a new heart*

*Psalm 42:3, 5, 42:3, 4 Like the deer that yearns for running streams, so my soul is yearning for you, my God*

*Romans 6:3–11 Christ once raised from the dead will never die again*

*Psalm 117:1–2, 16–17, 22–23 Alleluia, alleluia, alleluia!*

*Luke 24:1–12 Why are you looking for the living among the dead?*

The Easter Vigil was just drawing to a close and the congregation was about to sing the wonderful hymn 'Christ the Lord Is Risen Today' when the church doors were flung open and three or four young people from the local estate ran into the back of the church. People looked round to see where the noise had come from. The youngsters began to laugh and then bellowed at the top of their voices 'We wish you a merry Christmas, we wish you a merry Christmas and a happy new year' before running off, laughing loudly and slamming doors as they left. I recall the joyful proclamation of the resurrection in song was preceded by a few mutterings and 'Tut-tuts' about 'young people'.

Holy Saturday can seem strange enough even without Christmas songs at the end of it. Although there is no liturgy until darkness has fallen, there is a great sense of preparation, and in parishes throughout the country flowers will be filling the churches once again. In the past, the Vatican has had a team of florists on hand to arrange the 30,000 tulips, daffodils, roses and orchids – not to forget the 3-foot-high delphiniums – which are a gift from the Netherlands,

But Holy Saturday is not about flower displays. The Easter Vigil is a mini history lesson, that of salvation, as the Old Testament readings remind us of God's plan from creation through the sacrifice of Isaac to the crossing of the Red Sea and the messages of the prophets with that wonderful image from Ezekiel: 'I shall pour clean water over you and you will be cleansed; I shall cleanse you of all your filth and of all your foul idols. I shall give you a new heart and put a new spirit in you; I shall remove the heart of stone from your bodies and give you a heart of flesh … You will be my people and I shall be your God' (Ezek. 36: 25–26, 28).

There is wonderful symbolism in light gradually seeping into a darkened church: 'Christ our Light!' But this day is not just symbolic. Holy Saturday is not re-enacting stories from long ago. It is celebrating the resurrection of Jesus because here is life – light shining in our daily lives.

To the young people from the estate, the truth is that there would be no Christmas without Easter. The Bethlehem baby would have just been another little baby were it not for the passion, death and resurrection he experienced, which he underwent on our behalf. Happy Easter – and Happy Christmas!

*Something strange is happening — there is a great silence on earth today, a great silence and stillness. The whole earth keeps silence because the King is asleep. The earth trembled and is still because God has fallen asleep in the flesh and He has raised up all who have slept ever since the world began. God has died in the flesh and hell trembles with fear.*

*He has gone to search for our first parent, as for a lost sheep. Greatly desiring to visit those who live in darkness and in the shadow of death (Luke 1:79), He has gone to free from sorrow the captives Adam and Eve, He who is both God and the son of Eve.*

*The Lord approached them bearing the cross, the weapon that had won Him the victory. At the sight of Him, Adam, the first man He had created, struck his breast in terror and cried out to everyone: 'My Lord be with you all.' Christ answered him: 'And with your spirit.' He took him by the hand and raised him up, saying: 'Awake, O sleeper, and rise from the dead, and Christ will give you light.'*

From an ancient homily on Holy Saturday

**What Holy Saturday message would you give to a stranger?**

# EASTER WEEK

# EASTER SUNDAY

*According to a 2019 YouGov poll, the Cadbury Creme Egg is the most famous confectionery in the UK. It is also the best-selling, with sales in excess of 200 million between Christmas and Easter, a period known as 'Creme Egg season'. The Creme Egg was first introduced in 1963 and was sold as Fry's Creme Egg. It was renamed in 1971 and 1.5 million are manufactured each day at the Cadbury's Bournville factory in Birmingham.*

*Acts 10:34, 37–43 We ate and drank with him after he rose from the dead*

*Psalm 118:1–2, 16–17, 22–23 This is the day the Lord has made; let us rejoice and be glad in it*

*Colossians 3:1–4 You must look for the things that are above, where Christ is*

*John 20:1–9 He must rise from the dead*

A common criticism of many religious beliefs and practices is that religion is just not relevant anymore. It is not cool and trendy. Relevance appears to be an all-important criterion, especially with young people. Perhaps it is a bit like street credibility. For over twenty years, an ecumenical network in the UK has been creating Christmas and Easter adverts – posters, radio commercials and short videos – to communicate the Christian message. The posters might appear on bus shelters and the like, trying to catch people's attention at important times in the Christian calendar, to show that the message is still relevant today.

For Easter 1995, the advert was a brightly-coloured poster with the words 'Surprise! said Jesus to his friends three days after they buried him.' As one eagle-eyed critic observed in a letter to a national newspaper, if you consult the Greek New Testament, Jesus' first word after rising from the dead was not 'surprise'.

But the resurrection is a surprise. Today, the churches celebrate a new dawn, a new beginning. Even those Easter eggs, which have been available in the shops since the end of December, have their religious links. In the Persian

Empire centuries before the birth of Christ it was believed the two contending forces in the world were good and evil, Ormuzd and Ahriman. The egg was the bone of contention between the opposing forces and it was associated with death and rebirth. At the start of the new year, people would give each other eggs as symbol of life and fertility. As in many cultures and religions, the Church adopted this ancient custom, with the egg seen as a symbol of the resurrection. There was also the tradition of painting eggs red, signifying the blood shed by Christ on the Cross to redeem us.

The gospel presents us with the dramatic discovery of the empty tomb. 'They have taken the Lord out of the tomb and we do not know where they have put him' (John 20:2), says Mary of Magdala. The empty tomb is a surprise to Jesus' friends 'who had still not understood the scripture, that he must rise from the dead' (20:9). As we know, Jesus had not been 'put' anywhere. He rose to give new life to us. That is a surprise worth celebrating, and not just with Easter eggs, but every day of our lives.

*Easter challenges us each year. Do we believe that Christ truly rose from the dead? Belief in Christ's Resurrection is fundamental and essential to being a Christian.*

*Christianity makes demands. It is not an easy option. Its founder, Jesus Christ, called for a change of heart, a turning to God. He demanded a change in ways of thinking and in behaviour. That call is still being made to us in our day. Shall we listen to it?*

*We have the same duty [as the apostles] to give witness to the fact that Christ is risen from the dead. Death has lost its hold over mankind. Death is not, for us, the end of the story. It is the beginning of a new chapter. There is life after death; it is a life with God. Our present life is to prepare for that.*

Cardinal George Basil Hume, 1923–1999

**What does the 'new life' of Easter mean to you?**

# EASTER MONDAY

*The traditional Italian Colomba di Pasqua, a sweet bread cake made from dough and shaped like a dove, is also covered in pearl sugar and studded with almonds. There are a number of legends about its origins. One tradition dates back to the year 612 and the northern Italian city of Pavia, at the time the capital of the Lombards. The Irish Saint Columbanus arrived in the city with his disciples and they were welcomed by Queen Theodelinda, who provided a royal banquet. Since it was the season of Lent, St Columbanus and his disciples declined to eat meat. The queen was offended, and so St Columbanus attempted to appease his host by saying that they could not eat the meat until it had been blessed. As he raised his right hand in blessing, the meat turned into white bread loaves shaped like doves.*

*Acts 2:14, 22–23 God raised this man Jesus to life, and of that we are all witnesses*

*Psalm 16:1–2, 5, 7–11 Preserve me, O God, for in you I take refuge*

*Matthew 28:8–15 Go and tell my brothers that they must leave for Galilee; there they will see me*

A priest in Rome used to begin Easter Monday Mass with the words '*Buona Pasqua continua*' – 'Happy ongoing Easter'. In Italy, Easter Monday is called *La Pasquetta*, 'Little Easter', or *Lunedì dell'Angelo*, 'Monday of the Angel', remembering the two Marys who discovered the empty tomb and were comforted by angels. It is a day of rest and relaxation, and, weather permitting, an opportunity to head to the hills for a picnic with friends. The Italians have a saying, '*Natale con i tuoi. Pasqua con chi vuoi*' – 'Christmas with your family. Easter with whomever you please'. The *Pasquetta* meal would include eggs, perhaps hard-boiled or coloured and baked in a special Italian Easter bread, and pasta, quiche, salami, cheeses … and nice wine, of course!

A picnic like this under the warm sun sounds the perfect way to continue Easter celebrations. 'We are the Easter people and alleluia is our song!' said Saint Pope John Paul II. Such enthusiasm almost jumps out of the gospel pages, which talk of the women filled 'with awe and great joy' (Matt. 28:8) as they 'ran' to tell the disciples about the message of the angels. Awe, great joy, running to tell others: how eloquently, and how challengingly, do these words speak to us about proclaiming the news of the resurrection not just then, but even more so now.

There are those who find the idea of resurrection uncomfortable and perhaps hope the whole story will go away. The chief priests and elders in the gospel pay what today we would call 'hush money' to achieve just that – hide any resurrection story. Eyewitnesses, then, were paid to keep quiet. But proclaiming the joy of the resurrection is a task for all Christians today, for Easter is an ongoing celebration.

*On this festive Monday, known as 'Monday of the Angel', the Liturgy resounds the announcement of the Resurrection proclaimed yesterday: 'Christ is Risen, Hallelujah!' In today's Gospel passage, we can hear the echo of the words the Angel addressed to the women who had hastened to the sepulchre: 'Then go quickly and tell his disciples that he has risen' (Matt. 28:7). We feel as if this invitation is also directed to us; to 'hasten' and to 'go' announce to the men and women of our times this message of joy and hope, of certain hope, because from the dawn of the third day, Jesus who was crucified, is raised. Death no longer has the last word. Life does! This is our certainty.*

*May the Virgin Mary, silent witness of the death and Resurrection of her Son Jesus, help us to be clear signs of the Risen Christ amid the affairs of the world, so that those who suffer tribulation and difficulties do not fall victim to pessimism, defeat, and resignation, but find in us many brothers and sisters who offer them support and solace. May our Mother help us to believe firmly in the Resurrection of Jesus: Jesus is Risen; He is alive here among us and this is a worthy mystery of salvation with the ability to transform hearts and life.*

Pope Francis, 17 April 2017

**Do you convey the news of the resurrection eagerly and with great joy?**

# EASTER TUESDAY

The State Coach of the Lord Mayor of London is one of the oldest ceremonial vehicles in the world still in regular use. The coach was commissioned in 1757 and cost £850. It is built mainly of wood and the body of the coach is attached to the undercarriage by four thick leather straps. The coach is highly decorated with ornaments and carvings and was described in 1805 as 'one of the most splendid baubles that ever amused the great children of this world or set the crowd agape'. The coach is housed in the Museum of London and at the Lord Mayor's Show is pulled by six shire horses.

*Acts 2:36–41 Repent and every one of you must be baptised in the name of Jesus Christ*

*Psalm 33:4–5, 18–20, 22 The Lord's merciful love fills the earth*

*John 20:11–18 I have seen the Lord and he has spoken to me*

I have never been to the Lord Mayor's Show in London, the annual parade through the streets after the inauguration of the mayor. The event dates back to 1215 when King John granted a charter allowing the citizens of London to elect their own mayor. One of the conditions he laid down was that the mayor had to travel from the City of London to swear loyalty to the Crown. The parade used to take place each year on the Feast of St Simon and St Jude, 28 October, but now takes places on the second Saturday in November. Today, the Lord Mayor's Show is three-mile procession featuring floats, marching bands and two giant wicker figures, Gog and Magog, the ancient guardians of London.

But – unambiguously stating the obvious – 'after the Lord Mayor's Show comes the dung-cart'. After the ceremonial parade and the pageantry comes the cleanup. This phrase was first used in the nineteenth century and today is used to refer to a sense of anticlimax or even disappointment after an exciting, impressive event.

So, Easter has ended, the Easter Monday bank holiday has been and gone, and everything is back to normal. The show is over, and it is back to how we were before. But this would be the case only if Easter made no difference. In the gospel account, Mary cannot really believe that everything has come to an end. She weeps at the empty tomb and even wants to know where the body is: 'Sir, if you have taken him away, tell me where you have put him, and I will take him away' (John 20:15). Even when she sees Jesus, she does not immediately realise it is him, and when she does she wants to cling to the past, to the Jesus figure she had known and followed, not the Risen Christ. 'Do not cling to me' is Jesus' message (20:17).

Easter day may have come and gone, but we must not grasp on to things as they used to be. We must not cling to the past. 'The promise is for you and your children, and for all those who are far away, for all those whom the Lord our God is calling to himself' (Acts 2:39). This promise, made to us, means things can never be the same again. The Lord is calling us.

*We are called not only to believe that Christ once rose from the dead, thereby proving that he was God; we are called to experience the Resurrection in our own lives by entering into his dynamic movement, following Christ who lives in us. This life, this dynamism, is expressed by the power of love and encounter: Christ lives in us if we love one another ... We have been called to share in the Resurrection of Christ not because we have fulfilled all the laws of God and man, not because we are religious heroes, but because we are suffering human beings, sinners fighting for our lives, prisoners fighting for freedom, rebels taking up spiritual weapons against the powers that degrade and insult our human dignity.*

Thomas Merton, 1915–1968

**After the celebration of Easter, what is new for you?**

# EASTER WEDNESDAY

*A signpost by the Canal de Castille, Spain, shows various religious destinations and their distances. It is on the route of the Camino de Santiago, the pilgrim route to the shrine of St James in Santiago de Compostela in northwest Spain.*

*Acts 3:1–10 I will give you what I have: in the name of Jesus Christ the Nazarene stand up and walk!*

*Psalm 105:1–4, 6–9 Let the hearts that seek the Lord rejoice*

*Luke 24:13–35 They recognised Jesus at the breaking of bread*

As a youngster, I decided (or maybe mum and dad told me) to give up sugar for Lent. This meant no more cups of tea with two spoonfuls. Since then, I have never had sugar in tea. So Lent worked! I still eat sweets and sugary things, and probably too many of them, but take no sugar in tea. So is this what it is all about? Learning how to survive without that ten grams of carbohydrates and twenty calories per day? The purpose of Lenten self-denial is not about curbing the excesses of a sweet tooth or a convenient stimulus to diet. The aim is not to shed a few unwanted pounds or to proudly boast of not having said 'Mine's a pint!' for a few weeks.

The well-known story of the disciples on the road to Emmaus is like the pieces of a jigsaw puzzle finally falling into place as we celebrate Easter, explaining what it is all about. The disciples had their own particular expectations ('he was the one to set Israel free', Luke 24:21), which appear to have been dashed, and so naturally they were downcast. But Jesus paints the picture for them by explaining the scriptures, and he does it in such a way that their 'hearts [burned] within us as he talked to us on the road and opened the scriptures to us' (24:32). Their journey to Emmaus, their journey of discipleship, can only lead to participation in the new life of Christ.

The exact location of Emmaus is unknown, but it

was linked by road to Jerusalem. The two disciples were so full of joy and life that they set out immediately to go and tell the others what had happened – that the Lord had truly risen. That is the point of Lent: to give us the joy, the certainty, the conviction and belief that the companion who has been with us throughout the journey is the Lord himself, for he calls us to walk with him in the new life that he brings. 'Let the hearts that seek the Lord rejoice' (Ps. 105:3).

*The locality of Emmaus has not been identified with certainty. There are various hypotheses and this one is not without an evocativeness of its own for it allows us to think that Emmaus actually represents every place: the road that leads there is the road every Christian, every person, takes. The Risen Jesus makes himself our travelling companion as we go on our way, to rekindle the warmth of faith and hope in our hearts and to break the bread of eternal life. In the disciples' conversation with the unknown wayfarer the words the evangelist Luke puts in the mouth of one of them are striking: 'We had hoped ...' (Luke 24:21). This verb in the past tense tells all: we believed, we followed, we hoped ... but now everything is over. Even Jesus of Nazareth, who had shown himself in his words and actions to be a powerful prophet, has failed, and we are left disappointed. This drama of the disciples of Emmaus appears like a reflection of the situation of many Christians of our time: it seems that the hope of faith has failed. Faith itself enters a crisis because of negative experiences that make us feel abandoned and betrayed even by the Lord. But this road to Emmaus on which we walk can become the way of a purification and maturation of our belief in God. Also today we can enter into dialogue with Jesus, listening to his Word. Today too he breaks bread for us and gives himself as our Bread. And so the meeting with the Risen Christ that is possible even today gives us a deeper and more authentic faith tempered, so to speak, by the fire of the Paschal Event; a faith that is robust because it is nourished not by human ideas but by the Word of God and by his Real Presence in the Eucharist.*

Pope Benedict XVI, 6 April 2008

Have there been times in your Lenten journey when you have felt enlightened and comforted by the Lord's presence?

# Epilogue

The easy way to end this book is to write a few trite words. 'I hope you enjoyed this Lenten journey … Thank you for reading right to the end (unless you are one of those people who picks up a book and reads the last page first) … I hope it was more worthwhile than giving up chocolate biscuits …' and so on.

That would be wrong. Lent is not the end but the start, or an opportunity to begin again. 'Lent is a journey that involves our whole life, our entire being,' said Pope Francis. 'It is a time to reconsider the path we are taking, to find the route that leads us home and to rediscover our profound relationship with God, on whom everything depends.'

I hope that like the disciples on the road to Emmaus your journey through Lent and the start of Eastertide has helped you to rediscover or has enhanced your relationship with God, who comes to meet us in Jesus. After a true encounter with the Risen Lord, we can never be the same again.

Let us end our reflections with the words of Thomas Merton.

*We often forget that in all the accounts of the Resurrection, the witnesses started out with the unshakeable conviction that Christ was dead. The women going to the tomb thought of Jesus as dead and gone …*

*Now this is a kind of psychological pattern for the way we too often act in our Christian lives. Though we may still say with our lips that Christ is risen, we secretly believe him, in practice, to be dead. And we believe that there is a massive stone blocking the way and keeping us from getting to his dead body …*

*Such Christianity is no longer life in the Risen Christ, but a formal cult of the dead Christ, considered not as the Light and Saviour of the world, but as a kind of divine 'thing', an extremely holy object, a theological relic …*

*We must never let our religious ideas, customs, rituals and conventions become more real to us than the Risen Christ. We must learn with St Paul that all these religious accessories are worthless if they get in the way of our faith in Jesus Christ, or prevent us from loving our brothers and sisters in Christ. Paul looked back on the days when he had been a faultless observer of religious law, and confessed that all this piety was meaningless. He rejected it as worthless. He wanted one thing only. Here are his words … 'All I want to know is Christ in the power of his Resurrection, and to share his sufferings by reproducing the pattern of his death' (Philippians 3:11).*

# References

All scripture texts are taken from *Revised New Jerusalem Bible Study Edition* (London: Darton, Longman & Todd, 2019).

# ACKNOWLEDGEMENTS

I would like to thank David Moloney and all his colleagues at Darton, Longman and Todd for encouraging me to start writing once again. My sincere gratitude goes to Ted Harrison, whose artistic creative genius – and patience – has enriched the work. Thank you! And to Patricia, whose constant love and support makes all the difference.